All Black
and
Amber

All Black
and
Amber

1963 and a Game of Rugby

STEVE LEWIS

First impression: 2013

© Copyright Steve Lewis and Y Lolfa Cyf., 2013

The contents of this book are subject to copyright, and may
not be reproduced by any means, mechanical or electronic,
without the prior, written consent of the publishers.

Cover design: Y Lolfa
Cover photograph: *South Wales Evening Post*

ISBN: 978 184771 738 2

FSC

Published and printed in Wales
on paper from well maintained forests by
Y Lolfa Cyf., Talybont, Ceredigion SY24 5HE
website www.ylolfa.com
e-mail ylolfa@ylolfa.com
tel 01970 832 304
fax 832 782

Acknowledgements

To WRITE ABOUT a game of rugby that took place 50 years ago requires much help from various quarters. Without the input of those who played in the match there would not have been a book, and I must first thank the Newport players who gave so readily of their time and showed no small amount of patience when I rang to clarify some final detail. They are: Ray Cheney, Ian Ford, Neville Johnson, Brian Jones, David Jones, Dennis Perrott, Keith Poole, Brian Price, Bob Prosser, Algy Thomas, Dick Uzzell, David Watkins and Stuart Watkins. I am also grateful to Brian Cresswell who was more than happy to talk about a time that remains the great disappointment in his long and distinguished playing career.

One point I must clarify is that after such a long period of time there were, understandably, occasions during the interviewing process when opinions were seen to differ on certain issues. The players are together in their recollection of the match and other events that took place on the day, but gave varying accounts of some less important details. If such differences of opinion could not be resolved by going with a majority, then I have been swayed by either comments in the press, written works or simply by following my own instincts.

At the Welsh Rugby Union, Peter Owens was always on hand to help with any queries and allowed me access to the bowels of the Millennium Stadium wherein lies a wealth of historical documentation of enormous interest to the researcher. At the reference department of Newport Central Library thanks are due to Alex Jarvis and the team who, after so many visits, continue to wonder at my inability to get the reels on the microfiche and why I always look lost when making my way around the facility in search of the various information required.

The Friends of Newport Rugby do a fantastic job and I must wholeheartedly recommend anybody looking for the minutiae of Newport RFC to visit www.historyofnewportrugby.co.uk where all will be revealed. Thanks go individually to Kevin Jarvis, Graham Sully, Steve Bennett and Mike Dams – keep up the good work.

While enjoying the company of several former players at their regular match day functions, I was ever on the look out for any information, any snippet of gossip that might prove to be of use. Unwitting participants as they undoubtedly were, thanks must go to: Doug Ackerman, John Anderson, Tom Baxter-Wright, Jim Brunnock, Ron Davies (sadly now deceased), Angus Evans, Des Greenslade, Gordon Keeley, Haydn Mainwaring, Bryn Meredith, Bobby Owen, Ewart Prior, Peter Rees, Jeff Watkins, Paul Watts and Richie Wills. Apologies for any omissions.

Phil Webb on the sports desk at the *South Wales Argus* helped me get a request printed in the paper inviting anybody who was at the match and had an interesting story to tell to make contact. Many thanks to those who responded with their recollections of the day, in particular Howard Gabe Davies and Clive Wood whose tales are recounted in the text.

The team at Y Lolfa have maintained their usual high standards and particular mention must go to Lefi Gruffudd who embraced the project from the start. Clearly he wanted to redress the balance after being involved in a publication to celebrate Llanelli's great day in 1972. I hope I have got my argument across without treading on too many toes west of the Loughor! Similarily, Eirian Jones proved to be an editor who showed great understanding of the subject matter and my efforts to reach beyond a game of rugby. Many thanks.

My old friend Keith Erickson was with me on the terrace

behind the posts when Dick Uzzell dropped for glory. We also sat together in the front row of the stalls at the Capital Cinema in Cardiff when the Beatles played the venue in December 1965. How we got the tickets is a long story but Keith is a constant source of encouragement and a sounding board for some of my hare-brained ideas. I shudder to think what this book might have been called if not for his down to earth attitude.

Every effort has been made to identify the original sources of the photographs and I extend apologies for any inadvertent breach of copyright.

Many readers will be surprised to know that my long-suffering wife, Catherine, still puts up with my search for a good rugby story and in *All Black and Amber* I believe I have found another to add to the list. Contrary to Frank Zappa's comments regarding rock journalism which, he said "…is people who can't write, interviewing people who can't talk for people who can't read…", I know I interviewed people who can talk and am confident that whoever is holding this book can read. All that remains is for others to judge whether I can write but I gave it my best shot and I hope that my love of the Beatles is not too obvious!

Steve Lewis
October 2013

Contents

Introduction

"Sexual intercourse began
In nineteen sixty-three..."
Philip Larkin (1922–85)

B IG YEAR 1963. Same number of days and weeks as any other, barring those leap years which arrive in a four-year cycle and boast an extra day in February, but history tells us that 1963 stands out as one of the landmark years of the 20th century. From an early age dates such as that of the Battle of Hastings in 1066, the Great Fire of London in 1666, the Battle of Trafalgar in 1805 and the Battle of Waterloo in 1815 are all retained somewhere in the memory bank and when we arrive at the 20th century many others are to be found. Those marking the outbreak of World War I in 1914 and World War II in 1939, for example. Following the death of her father King George VI, Queen Elizabeth II acceded to the throne in 1952 and was crowned in 1953, the same year that Sir Edmund Hillary became the first man to reach the summit of Mount Everest. More recent years saw England's footballers win the World Cup in 1966, Neil Armstrong be the first man to walk on the moon in 1969 and the death of Elvis Presley in 1977 followed three years later by the shooting of John Lennon. All are dates that kick-start the grey matter, dates that immediately bring to mind the sometimes earth shattering events together with the happier occasions.

So what is it about 1963 that suggests it should be remembered in isolation, not just considered as part of a decade or more generally a small window in the latter part of the 20th century? Quite simply, 1963 embraced events both within Britain and beyond that ensured it would become one of the most studied and discussed years in living memory. Fifty years on is as good a time as any to reflect on a year that began with Britain covered in a blanket of snow and ice, the severity of which had not been witnessed for 200 years, and ended with the nation strutting around to a new sound, one that would herald monumental changes in the way we thought and the way we behaved. The recognised establishment, which had pretty much ruled the thumb over how the country was run, would be rocked on its heels, bounced off the ropes and finally beaten into submission.

Between the snow and the new-found spring in the heel, Britain saw a change at Number 10 Downing Street, a new leader of the opposition party, and a political scandal that was at the same time both embarrassing to the Government and was played to full advantage by the other side of the House. The eventual resignation of the Secretary of State for War, John Profumo, brought to an end a saga that had fed off speculation regarding who had slept with whom and the content of the subsequent pillow talk. Neither did a restructuring of the railway network win Prime Minister Harold Macmillan any friends. Dr Richard Beeching's proposals were not well received by a public still looking to move on from the legacy of World War II and the austerity of the 1950s. For some there were alternatives, and when the Glasgow to London mail train was hijacked in August it was the biggest robbery on record and dominated the headlines for many weeks. The Profumo Affair and the Great Train Robbery would never be forgotten. A number of books and films ensure that they remain in the public domain proving that, for some at least, infamy and crime does indeed pay, even if not for the perpetrators themselves.

The biggest headline of the twelve months was delivered when the 35th president of the United States was assassinated on 22 November. John F. Kennedy had captured the imagination and hopes of a nation in his short term in office and much was expected of the charismatic Democrat. Earlier in the year Martin Luther King had addressed a huge gathering at the Lincoln Memorial in Washington. This was the culmination of a civil rights march supported by an estimated 250,000 people and his 'I have a dream...' speech is one of the most famous and referenced of the 20th century. Already serving a prison term for indictment, Nelson Mandela appeared in a Pretoria courthouse at the end of the year to face charges of treason which would result in a life sentence and see him incarcerated for 27 years before his eventual release in 1990.

The year also welcomed a new pontiff, Giovanni Battista Montini elected as Pope Paul VI succeeding the recently deceased Pope John XXIII. French President Charles de Gaulle vetoed Britain's entry into the Common Market, Kim Philby went missing from Beirut and if this was all too much to take on board light relief arrived in the shape of William Hartnell as *Dr Who*, the cult BBC television programme making its debut on 23 November.

Politics and criminal activity aside, 1963 is also remembered as the year that saw popular music and popular culture change social attitudes and perceptions forever. While the Beatles were leading the assault on the senses at home a young troubadour from Duluth, Minnesota in the USA was pricking the conscience of a generation in search of itself. With songs such as 'Blowin in the Wind', 'Masters of War' and 'A Hard Rain's a-Gonna Fall', Bob Dylan proved essential listening. The protest song had arrived but for John, Paul, George and Ringo life appeared to be much more straightforward. There were no thought-provoking lyrics to be had from this Liverpool foursome, rather songs that reflected adolescent love in all its simplicity, singalong numbers that swept all before them. With their repetitive oohs and yeah, yeah, yeahs, 'Please, Please Me', 'From Me To You', 'She Loves You' and 'I Want to Hold Your Hand' were both immediate and unforgettable.

Philip Larkin continued that sexual intercourse not only '...Began in nineteen sixty-three...' but more specifically

'...Between the end of the "Chatterley" ban / And the Beatles first LP.' All of which perfectly captures the mood of the nation in a handful of words. That they were written a decade later is not significant but the title of the poem from which they are extracted is 'Annus Mirabilis' – remarkable year – and so it was. There may have been far too many black days but these were balanced by some extraordinary achievements, days when you had to stand back and pinch yourself to make sure that perhaps this wasn't part of some dream from which you would soon wake up. One such occasion took place on 30 October at a rugby ground in south Wales; at Rodney Parade, Newport to be more precise.

This book is about that day, the events that led up to it and those that followed. It is a book about a rugby match, 80 minutes of sport that saw 30 men stand up and be counted. It is perhaps inconceivable that a book about a game of rugby should invite the likes of John Lennon, Ronnie Biggs, Ena Sharples, Clint Eastwood and Rolf Harris onto its pages. Nor would the reader expect to find room made for Jack Ruby, Stephen Ward, the Shadows, Alec Douglas-Home, Harold Wilson, Pinky and Perky or Benny Hill. These are names one would normally pursue elsewhere but, by bringing them together with many more of similar virtue and notoriety, it is hoped that the flavour of the time in question and the nostalgia it continues to inspire will help depict a year of historical importance way beyond the parameters of the oval ball.

Most of the events that dominated 1963 have their own place in history and are well documented accordingly but the game of rugby football that took place on 30 October has yet to receive the attention it deserves. Now, on the occasion of its 50th anniversary, it is appropriate that the extraordinary performance of 15 men should be revisited, reassessed and given its proper place in the annals of Welsh rugby. Such unique sporting occasions and the names of those involved in them are in great danger of being erased from the landscape, remembered only by the small and ever decreasing numbers who remain focussed on the task of spreading the word but who sadly, one suspects, are fighting a losing battle. We are part of a society that lives for the moment, everyone in search of their 15 minutes of fame and to hell with the consequences. Henry Ford was wrong. History isn't more or less bunk; rather it is essential to the way things are viewed in later years which is why the baton must be passed down through successive generations and the grand tales of yesteryear told and retold, even if they might be embellished a little along the way. All of which grants us license to focus attention on those 80 minutes of rugby football and the men in black and amber jerseys who did stand up to be counted. This is their story.

CHAPTER ONE

When Rugby Came Second

"I'm dreaming of a white Christmas..."
Irving Berlin (1888–1989)

IT STARTED IN Scotland. Snow arrived in the Highlands on 22 December 1962 and slowly but relentlessly began working its way south. Nothing unusual seeing the white stuff in late December; many would argue that it is part and parcel of the festive season and bemoan its absence if none were to fall, but the innocent looking flakes that fell over much of Britain during the next few days would herald the start of a winter set to test the resolve of the hardiest individuals and go on record as the worst for 200 years.

The snow didn't reach south Wales in time for Christmas Day. There were no snowmen to be made, snowballs to be thrown or tobogganing to be enjoyed at the risk of life and limb but there would be plenty of time for such diversions in the weeks and months ahead. No, Christmas Day in Newport was a quiet time – peace and goodwill to all men etc. There were birds to be stuffed, vegetables to be prepared. The Christmas pudding had probably been made well in advance and somewhere in its rich depths were sure to be found the odd sixpenny piece or two. Christmas cakes were decorated in thick white icing, circled by a glitzy cummerbund with a couple of festive characters positioned on top and there would certainly be mince pies, sherry, nuts and fruit. Fifty years may have passed but little has changed in the fare served up at the Christmas Day dinner table. It has always provided the opportunity for an almighty 'blow out' which few pass on – all good diets start on 1 January!

Fed and watered it would then be the time to fall asleep in front of the black and white television. Hardly a new addition to domesticity, but in the early 1960s television remained very much in its infancy with the choice of channels numbering only two. In 1962 the BBC's offerings included a visit to *Billy Smart's Christmas TV Circus*, a staged pantomime which that year was *Puss in Boots*, Leonard Sachs presenting *The Good Old Days*, and the night ended with Humphrey Bogart and Katherine Hepburn aboard *The African Queen*, a film that had played in cinemas ten years earlier. If none of that appealed the commercial channel ITV offered an alternative. Here the prime slots were filled by *Discs a Go-Go*, *Emergency – Ward 10* and an hour in the company of Dickie Henderson. Then it was a rendition of 'God Save the Queen' before the screen faded to a dot.

On Boxing Day Stratford Johns, Colin Welland and Brian Blessed chased the villains in *Z-Cars*, the popular BBC police drama which was followed by *Benny Hill* and *Whicker's World*. Among ITV's offerings was a trip down *Coronation Street* which is still going strong, although Ena Sharples, Martha Longhurst and Minnie Caldwell have long since stopped supping milk stout in the snug. Music, dance and comedy were in the safe hands of Norman Vaughan and Bruce Forsyth and the evening could wind up with a trip out west following the escapades of Rowdy Yates played by a youthful Clint Eastwood in the popular *Rawhide*. And if none of that cornucopia of entertainment appealed then it was time to crank up the Dansette record player, stack the 45s, hope they dropped one at a time, get granny on her feet and have a bop.

In the early 1960s, people looking to pick up the latest

musical hits in Newport could head for W.H. Smith in the High Street, Woolworths on Commercial Street or there was the Music Centre. Found in Skinner Street, opposite the Olympia cinema, owner Maurice White's Music Centre was a mecca for both musical instruments and records. That it was the preferred choice of most adolescent schoolboys probably had more to do with the talents of Jan, she of the beehive hair and the horn-rimmed glasses. Jan would send prospective customers to one of the listening booths at the back of the shop and play any record of choice – sold! Discs came in three formats, the long player (LP), an extended play (EP), and singles. The Top 40 was the domain of the singles with the best-selling discs of the week vying for the coveted number one, the peak of a recording artist's career.

Christmas 1962 saw Elvis Presley topping the charts with 'Return to Sender', Cliff Richard and the Shadows would have to wait another week before the double-sided 'The Next Time'/ 'Bachelor Boy' could claim the number one spot. That chart for the week ending 27 December makes interesting reading. While Brenda Lee was 'Rockin' Around the Christmas Tree' and Susan Maughan was yearning to be 'Bobby's Girl', Frank Ifield had the 'Lovesick Blues', Rolf Harris was watching the 'Sun Arise' and Mark Wynter couldn't get enough of his 'Venus in Blue Jeans'. Then there were the instrumentals: The Shadows with 'Dance On!'; 'Telstar' by the Tornados; Joe Loss and his Orchestra found favour with 'Must Be Madison'; and the John Barry Orchestra had scored with the James Bond theme to *Dr No*, a tune most people on the planet are still familiar with 50 years on.

And at number 17, up from the previous weeks number 22, was a tune celebrating its ninth week in the charts but would not get any higher until October 1982 when, on its re-release, it reached number four. For what extended to a 14-week stay in the Top 40 best-selling singles, most of Liverpool must have bought copies of the first recording by a little known group who would rewrite the record books appertaining to all things musical and in so doing help change social demographics forever. Sandwiched between 'The Main Attraction' by Pat Boone and Hank Locklin's 'We're Gonna Go Fishing' was 'Love Me Do' by The Beatles. Not the group's most memorable effort but neither was it their worst. But it was their first, it got them up and running and for that we have to be eternally grateful.

Christmas Day fell on a Tuesday in 1962. For many this meant a long break from work during which they would be looking for something to get them out of the house, an excuse to get some fresh air in the lungs, stretch the legs. The fixture secretary at Newport Rugby Football Club must have welcomed the opportunity to arrange for three home matches to be played during the holiday period: Watsonians, the traditional Boxing Day opponents from north of the border would be at Rodney Parade on Wednesday afternoon; the Universities Athletic Union (UAU) had agreed to get a team to Newport for an evening fixture under the floodlights on Thursday; and on Saturday the RAF would bring the curtain down on the first half of the 1962–3 season.

And what a first half of the campaign it had been but memorable it certainly wasn't. Between 1 September and 29 December, Newport had lost eleven and drawn two of the 25 games played. Only once before had the famous club experienced such miserable form when losing twelve of the 19 outings before the turn of the year. That was back in 1932–3 under the captaincy of Raymond Ralph, who had to try and rally the troops as bad became worse in the new year, his team losing 13 of the 14 matches played in the last two months of a wretched season. Statistical information can always be used to advantage, or otherwise, but 30 years on from that disappointing campaign Newport did improve on its early form. In the second half of the season the club won 14 and drew one of the 17 matches played during March and April which, as we shall see, represented the remaining fixtures in a campaign greatly disrupted by meteorological events. Nobody could possibly have forecast that those three matches played over the Christmas holiday would be the last at the ground until 13 March, barring one important exception. That aside, Newport RFC had certainly played its last match at Rodney Parade for what amounted to the thick end of eleven weeks.

So how did the club fare during the festive period? With adverse weather reports suggesting the snow and cold weather would reach the area some time over the holiday, precautions were taken and the pitch was covered with straw on Christmas Eve. Officials at the club were fully aware that the Watsonians, in particular, had a long journey south and a late cancellation was to be avoided if at all possible. Twelve months earlier there had been a similar scenario, with several tons of straw placed on a freezing pitch in an effort to make it playable come Boxing Day. On that occasion the elements were in control, the visitors of the opinion that the ground was far too hard, resulting in the cancellation of the match. There was to be no repeat in 1962. The straw did its job and, after clearing the pitch, conditions underneath proved acceptable to both teams and the referee was able to give the go-ahead. The Watsonians defeated Newport 8–6, the eleventh loss of the season, and no sooner had the players left the field than the covering of straw was replaced in the hope that it would provide enough warmth to prevent the ground freezing overnight.

The first of the promised snow fell in the small hours making the task of removing the cover more difficult but when the call for help was heard, hundreds of supporters turned up at the ground to assist in raking off the snow and straw and Thursday night's fixture with the UAU was on. Newport beat the students 14–8 and on Saturday the RAF were defeated 22–3 after another laudable effort from the ground staff and volunteers. Two out of three ain't bad as the song goes, but it is certain that all involved at Newport RFC were glad to see the back of 1962, the stalwart efforts of the team in the early part of the year when only two of 24 matches were lost nothing but a distant memory.

Club captain and international back row forward, Glyn Davidge, was manfully trying to steady the ship at Rodney Parade as 1962 drew to a close. The previous season, hooker Bryn Meredith was captain, and under his astute leadership Newport had performed well, particularly at home where only Abertillery had claimed the spoils with a close fought 8–6 victory. Meredith was one of Welsh rugby's outstanding players of the post-war era. He won the last of 34 caps when leading Wales against Ireland in Dublin in March and spent much of that summer in South Africa on what was a third British Lions tour. On his return Meredith advised club officials that it was his intention to wind down a distinguished playing career and let some new blood take over. There would be a handful of appearances over the next three seasons but Bryn Meredith's major contribution to Newport RFC during the period would be made from the touchline.

A rugby club is something of a moveable feast. At the end of each season there will be those like Meredith who know the time has come to step down, take a back seat and let youth have its head. There will be others who leave in search of pastures new, players who may not have seen regular first-team rugby or who simply want a change of scenery. But there is always a balancing exercise, a case of out with the old and in with the new. Before the season gets under way many an aspiring player will approach the club in the hope of getting a run-out in a trial match, the pre-season showcases at which talent, or otherwise, is quickly recognised. One such trial match is a good place to begin the story of a team that would rewrite the record books at the club, register a one-off victory that would surpass all that had gone before and never be bettered. Among those hoping to impress in the preliminaries ahead of the 1961–2 season, impress Meredith and the other members of the selection committee, were six players who would not only pass the acid test but who were each destined to play a part in what would be Newport RFC's finest hour.

David Jones was a tight-head prop who had been playing for Bargoed in the Rhymney Valley, one of the many junior clubs found throughout Wales which were the very foundation of the club game and the recognised breeding ground of numerous players who would go on to greater things. In the modern game a good tight-head prop is an essential component of any team and a great one can be worth his weight in gold. Nothing standing less than six foot tall and weighing-in at upwards of 18 stone would satisfy the current criteria. Such specimens were not around in 1963 and, at a shade under six foot and weighing 14 stone ten pounds dripping wet, Jones was about par for the course among those monoliths of the front row who once looked so huge on the field of play. As he rightly says, David Jones would not be considered a big outside-half in the modern game.

After appearing in a trial at Cross Keys he decided to try his luck at Rodney Parade before making any commitment to a new club. The quality of player vying for a place in the Newport squad would have been higher than that encountered at Pandy Park, but Jones was clearly comfortable in such company and convinced the selection committee that he could be groomed to take over from the experienced Des Greenslade when that stalwart, now approaching his 30s, decided to call it a day. Greenslade had some gas left in the tank and the young pretender was limited to six first-team appearances in his first season and 13 in the second. The rest of the time he took his place in the front row of the club's second team, as good a place as any to hone one's playing skills, with Newport United playing a standard of rugby a level up from that with which he was familiar.

This was in marked contrast to the introduction to Newport

experienced by Alan 'Algy' Thomas. When the open-side wing forward elected to throw his lot in at Rodney Parade there would be no time spent with the United. Following his debut in the season's opening match against Penarth, Thomas played in every match – 44 consecutive appearances in total which, for a player in his first season at a club, must be some kind of record. Unlike Des Greenslade, flanker Geoff Whitson had decided to call it a day at the end of the previous season, and so the way was clear for Thomas to make his mark immediately, an opportunity he had no intention of failing to make the most of.

There is no doubting Algy Thomas' Welsh ancestry, but he first saw the light of day in Beckenham, Greater London. When the family eventually returned to Wales, the youngster found himself in a very different world to that which he had become familiar with in those early years, and it is difficult to imagine anywhere further removed from the environs of London than Pontlottyn, a small town at the head of the Rhymney Valley. From the local secondary school Thomas made his way south to Bargoed Technical School, where he studied engineering and had his first introduction to rugby football as a wing forward, a position which leant itself to the player's upper body strength and speed about the field. Word of mouth ensured Algy Thomas' ability reached beyond college rugby, and he was soon attracting the attention of local clubs. It was nearby Tredegar which secured his services, albeit not for long. Pontypool was his next port of call. In the demanding rugby arena that is Pontypool Park, Thomas proved that he really could step up to the plate, that he was comfortable playing at the higher level and that he was capable of going that bit further. A few short miles in fact, down the road to Newport where there was a big pair of boots that needed filling.

Another with connections to Bargoed, centre three-quarter John Uzzell, was already an international rugby player. The 19 year old represented Welsh Secondary Schools while a pupil at Bargoed Grammar School but during that summer of 1961 he was in transit, preparing to head off to St Luke's College, Exeter to study for a degree in physical education. Knowing that the college would have first call on his services for all Saturday matches, Uzzell was also aware that the holiday periods would be his own. So, best to get on the books at one of the local clubs. He joined David Jones in the pre-season trial at Cross Keys but like the prop forward, Uzzell was also destined to travel further down the valley. His first cousin, Brian Price, was playing for Newport at the time and it was Price who questioned Uzzell's logic in hoping to join Cross Keys even though he had played for the club himself and had fond memories of the time spent at Pandy Park. Price suggested that, apart from the kudos attached with playing for a bigger club, Newport would probably be more accommodating in paying his expenses if Uzzell were to be selected for any midweek matches.

Derived from *oiseau*, the French word for bird, Uzzell is not the most common of surnames but it was one already familiar to those with long memories. Harry Uzzell was a forward who won 15 Welsh caps between 1912–20, led his country on four occasions and captained Newport with some distinction in 1913–14. Now it was the turn of his great-nephew to represent the family name in the black and amber jersey. Christened John Uzzell he may well have been, but from an early age the moniker Dick had replaced John and would continue to do so. John Uzzell and his pals enjoyed playing on the many slag heaps that dotted the landscape and, after a few hours chasing the Indians or being chased by the cowboys, the young boy would return home covered from head to foot in soot and mud. It was his mother who first called him a Dirty Dick which his father, for whatever reason, reversed to Dicky Dirt. Whichever, the dirt could always be scrubbed off but Dick remained and will continue do so throughout the pages of this book.

Another about to make his mark at Rodney Parade was a wing three-quarter who may well have been born in Newport but, come 1961, was firmly entrenched in the Valleys, his family having relocated to Oakdale in the Sirhowy Valley when he was a lad. They say you can take the boy out of the Valleys but you can't take the Valleys out of the boy. Dennis Perrott was the compete reverse, a townie at heart despite the more rural environment in which he spent his formative years. Each season Perrott would eye the fixture lists with interest and if Newport had a home game he would set off down the valley on the local bus and wend his way to Rodney Parade to see his heroes play. This was during the 1950s when all roads seemed to lead to Rodney Parade on a Saturday. This was an era that witnessed some fine back play, the Newport three-quarters set alight by the genius of outside-half Roy Burnett, but it was the men out wide who Perrott followed with particular interest: John Lane, Graham Ross and the explosive Ken Jones, one of the quickest men ever to grace a rugby field.

Like Dick Uzzell, Dennis Perrott was another who chose to pursue a career in education and after two years National Service he started a teaching degree course at Cardiff College of Education. Within the small world that is Welsh rugby, Perrott also had a relative playing the game at one of the local clubs. In his case it was first cousin and Welsh international wing forward Haydn Morgan who introduced him to Abertillery RFC. Also at the club was number eight, Alun Pask, who would eventually join Morgan in the Welsh back row. Pask and Perrott had seen out their National Service together, so the college boy who had boasted some impressive times as a sprinter soon found himself scoring tries out wide in the green and white hoops of Abertillery.

Ambition and the desire to play for the club he followed as a young lad finally won over and after three seasons Dennis Perrott headed for Rodney Parade. His college course finished in June, by which time his intended move to Newport had been reported in the press. Lecturing at the college was Roy Bish who would later gain a reputation as a talented rugby coach.

25

Bish raised the subject with Perrott, questioning his change of club. Was it for the right reasons? Rugby union was a strictly amateur sport but rumours regarding under the table payments to players were not uncommon and maybe there was a case of no smoke without fire, but not in this instance. Bish was keen to point out that, of all the clubs, Newport had a reputation for adhering strictly to the book and if Perrott thought a change of club would have some financial reward, he was in for a shock. Perrott reassured him this was not the case and that his only interest was in playing the game at as high a level as possible. He felt Newport was the club that would offer him the best opportunity of doing so thereby giving Roy Bish the answer he wanted to hear.

The Valleys of south-east Wales were once world renowned for the production of coal and iron ore, but in 1961 it looked as if Newport RFC had come across a particularly rich seam of another kind. David Jones, Alan Thomas, Dick Uzzell and Dennis Perrott had all spent their formative years within a stone's throw of each other, and a short distance away lies the home of yet another player who joined the club that year. Navigate a couple of valleys east and you will stumble across Blaina, birthplace of David Watkins. Since the retirement of Roy Burnett and Malcolm Thomas, Newport had not found an outside-half to maintain the high standards set by these two former stars. Brian Jones came nearest to filling the gap but his rugby skills were undoubtedly best seen when he appeared in the centre. A new face was needed and it was the 19-year-old Watkins who was invited to take part in the pre-season trials, and he was immediately introduced into the team for the opening match of the 1961–2 season.

At the time, a certain amount of leeway was afforded to youth players before they joined a senior club. They were allowed to play up to four matches before having to make a commitment, the restriction not limited to one club. An outstanding prospect, Watkins had appeared for Blaina, Abertillery, Ebbw Vale and Pontypool during the previous season, but it was at Rodney

Parade that he set out his stall, and the next in a long line of Welsh outside-halves who would light up the game was on his way. Watkins readily admits that those early days at the club saw him taken out of his comfort zone. Coming from the close-knit community he was familiar with, life was about to change dramatically as he took the first steps of a career that would see him reach the heights not only in rugby union but also in the professional world of rugby league.

All outside-halves need a good partner. A good scrum-half who will ensure they get the ball they want, when they want it and where they want it. For the past two seasons Billy Watkins had been Newport's first-choice scrum-half. At 28 years of age Watkins was another player coming to the end of his career and the search began for an alternative, a younger man who could establish an efficient partnership with the new outside-half. This responsibility, over the coming seasons, would fall on the broad shoulders of Bob Prosser who was five months younger than his new partner. A product of Tylorstown in the Rhondda Valley, work had seen the family uproot and head for the Midlands when Prosser was barely three years old and he would not return to Wales for 15 years. It was at Bablake School in Coventry that Prosser got his first introduction to rugby, courtesy of a former player and a Welshman to boot. Gerwyn Morgan had played scrum-half for Swansea against the 1953 All Blacks when the club drew 6–6 with the tourists, and it was Morgan who recognised the basic skills required by all scrum-halves in the young Prosser: the ability to pass off either hand, a good kicking game, and an inherent awareness of everything going on around him.

The introduction to senior rugby came at Coventry where George Cole was the resident scrum-half. Prosser took his place in the seconds until the rare opportunities to play first-team rugby came his way. Accepted at UCW Cardiff, he finally returned to Wales, and it was while playing for the UAU against Newport on Easter Saturday 1961 that Prosser first came to the attention of the club's selection committee. The young scrum-half managed to impress in what was a heavy defeat for his team and Bob Prosser was invited to attend the trial matches held at Rodney Parade later that year.

The record books confirm the immediate impact these six players made. Alan Thomas played in all 44 matches, closely followed by David Watkins who made 39 appearances, one more than Dennis Perrott. Bob Prosser somehow managed to find the time to play in 29 matches and all but made the scrum-half position his own, despite the college having first call on his services. Dick Uzzell was less fortunate in that one of the centre berths was firmly in the hands of Brian Jones, and Exeter is much further from Newport than Cardiff, all of which limited him to 17 appearances. Of the six new faces David Jones' was the least familiar to those on the terraces come the end of the season, his task of gaining preference over the incumbent Des Greenslade a much different proposition. A regular for Newport United, his outings with the senior team numbered only six in that first season but David Jones knew that his day would come.

Further perusal of the records tells us that in the 1961–2 season centre Brian Jones, together with second-row forwards Ian Ford and Brian Price, each made 42 appearances; club captain and number eight Glyn Davidge led the team 35 times, with loose-head prop forward Neville Johnson playing in 34 matches. Further down the list we come across Graham Bevan, a first-class hooker who had spent five years as second choice behind Bryn Meredith. If David Jones ever felt he had made a bad decision when joining Newport, he need only have looked at the progress made by Bevan. Patience was the name of the game. Not deterred by the limited number of first-team appearances that came his way, the hooker bided his time, served his apprenticeship, watched and learnt, comfortable in the knowledge that age was on his side. With Meredith deciding to take a back seat, come September 1962 Graham Bevan was primed and ready to make his mark which he readily did. There may only have been seven first-team appearances in 1961–2 but twelve months on he featured in all bar two of the 42 matches played during a season turned on its head by the inclement weather.

It was to the Rodney Parade ground staff's eternal credit, together with help from an army of supporters, that Newport managed to fulfil the three fixtures over the Christmas holiday. Maybe it was with a degree of optimism that the covering of straw was put back in place following the match against the RAF but events dictated that there it would stay until further notice as the snow continued to fall across Britain. Nowhere escaped the white covering which got deeper and deeper as the days went by.

Come the new year the country was in the depths of some serious winter weather. Large parts of south-west England had been particularly badly affected with reports of winds raging at up to 90 m.p.h. causing 15 to 20 foot drifts and effectively cutting off many of the remote villages found in the area. With farmers unable to get their produce to market, much stock was ruined and, as a consequence, the vegetables that did appear on the grocers' shelves were sold at a premium. In Newport market local fruit and vegetable merchants Harry Wheeler and Sons even introduced rationing, such was the scarcity of the staple foodstuffs. Similarly, milk production was seriously affected and again this was reflected in the price and a not uncommon sight was that of milk bottles with their content bursting out of the top in a frozen frenzy.

Newport witnessed the same problems experienced the length and breadth of the country. Burst pipes caused horrendous problems for thousands which, in turn, led to people having to queue at hastily positioned stand pipes to collect a minimal supply of the water so essential to many domestic needs. There were power cuts, numerous road accidents and general chaos in the transport network that serviced the town and the all-important docks were closed for much of the time. Chaos reigned and nobody escaped the devastation brought about by the harmless looking white flakes that look so pretty as they wend their way to ground. To make any impression on the snow and ice, heavy plant machinery was needed and the whole situation was compounded when the reserves of diesel froze.

The inevitable knock-on effect saw industry and commerce grind to a halt as much of the workforce found itself unable to get to the factory or office. Schools were forced to close, largely as a consequence of deliveries of fuel needed to power the heating systems being unable to get through. In south Wales, the annual 11-plus examinations, which determined where pupils would continue their education come September, had to be postponed. But with the downside of not having to go to school, so too there was an upside. A plethora of snowmen appeared on the landscape, snowballs flew in every direction and purpose-built toboggans together with any other item that presented a smooth, flat surface carried one or more passengers down any incline that lent itself to the exercise.

Winter sports ruled and other than motorbike scrambling, which apparently thrived in the Arctic conditions, everything else was put on hold. Boxing Day saw only five First Division football matches played and thereafter it would be down to the Pools Panel to determine who would have beaten whom, be it home or away and where the much sought after draws were to be found. All horse racing was cancelled and it would be the end of February before there was a gradual resumption of fixtures.

A month into what was now being called the 'Big Freeze' warm air started to move in from the Atlantic and so began the slow process of thaw which in itself brought the additional threat of flooding. That was on 25 January, but four days later the snow returned with a vengeance and this second spate of winter weather would exceed all that had gone before. Again, the worst affected region was the south-west of England. Devon and Cornwall were cut off and throughout the country in excess of 200 major roads were reported as blocked and impassable with 130,000 miles of the network seriously affected. Neither was it any different on the railways, with many routes out of commission for much of the time. Air travel wasn't what we are familiar with in the 21st century but all major airports suffered severe disruption, something that is still endured 50 years on whenever the temperatures drop and the snow falls.

In today's currency £400 is a sizable amount to carry around in your wallet but in 1963 it bordered on a small fortune. A Mini Cooper could be put on the road for less than £600 and a new-build semi-detached property in Newport snapped up from a starting price of £2,750. When you have paid out £400 for a recording session at a leading studio in north London, inconveniences such as those produced by the adverse weather have to be overcome. On the morning of 11 February, the Beatles arrived at Abbey Road Studios with a bag full of songs and twelve hours in which to record them. The end result was 'Please, Please Me', the group's first long playing disc which ran to 14 numbers and would be released for public consumption on 22 March, marking the start of the greatest catalogue of music produced by any recording artists and the closure of Philip Larkin's timeframe for the introduction of the sexual revolution. The term Beatlemania, as the public response to the four lads from Liverpool would become known, was some months off but with 'Please, Please Me' the Beatles laid the foundation on which it would be built. It was heart-warming stuff but outside the studios, across the famous zebra crossing and beyond, Britain continued to freeze.

By way of explaining the freak weather conditions affecting all parts of the country, the public were informed that a combination of anticyclones from Siberia and Greenland had met over Britain and their combined impact forced the warm air that was coming from the south to rise above them. Apparently, these two weather fronts would normally arrive individually, allowing the warm air to gain the upper hand thus bringing about the thawing process – but not in 1963. Fingers were pointed in the search for a scapegoat which usually means those in officialdom. The last severe winter was as recent as 1947, but lessons had not been learnt, no precautions were put in place in the event that such extreme weather would revisit the British Isles. At £7,000 per unit, investment by local authorities in the appropriate equipment was viewed as excessive, a typical head in the sand scenario with which we are still familiar today.

Compared with the £15 million in insurance claims, the £20 million that needed to be invested repairing roads and the estimated £150–200 million costs run up in trying to keep the country functioning during January, February and into March, £7,000 on a digger seems small change. That aside, when it started to snow in late December, few could have anticipated still being inconvenienced as spring approached, but that was exactly what happened yet somehow, despite the frozen ground and the heavy falls of the white stuff, there was some rugby played.

The Five Nations Championship was scheduled to begin with Scotland travelling to Paris to play France on 12 January. This fixture was never under threat and Scotland got the season off to a promising start with a good victory away from home. The following Saturday, England were due to arrive in Cardiff for a match that at the turn of the year looked unlikely to take place. Before England could be entertained there was the small matter of the Welsh selectors picking a team to face them. The final trial had long since been scheduled to take place at St Helen's, Swansea on 5 January but this was never likely to happen. Hoping for some respite in the weather, the Welsh Rugby Union (WRU) optimistically moved the trial to the following Saturday but, by the start of the week, it was clear there was not going to be any improvement at St Helen's and with Cardiff Arms Park under a covering of straw, which itself was now under several feet of snow, using the international ground as an alternative venue was also ruled out – best leave the covering in place and only remove it on the day of the match if it went ahead.

With the trial now put back seven days, all that remained was to find a ground most likely to lend itself to the occasion. On Tuesday, 9 January, knowing that Newport had successfully staged three matches over Christmas, the WRU contacted the club with a view to playing the much needed final trial at Rodney Parade. It was going to take a massive effort to clear a pitch which was now lost beneath its covering of straw and snow. A labour-intensive exercise was the only remedy but, such was the Union's desire to ensure the best possible team was picked to face England and recognising the importance of the selectors having one final look at the leading candidates, it would underwrite all expenses incurred by the Newport club.

On a bitterly cold, miserable Saturday afternoon, 30 players in the guise of the Probables and Possibles served up some average fare for the hardy souls who had turned out for the game, and what the selectors actually gleaned from it is debatable. Regardless, they retired to the offices at Rodney Parade and, after having had their day further inconvenienced when a fire broke out, the Big Five duly announced the team that would face England. Two Newport players were selected. Brian Price was included in the second row to win his fifth cap and among six players due to make their international debut was outside-half, David Watkins. And if any Newport supporters wanted to see the pair represent their country against the old enemy, tickets were still available through the club. Grandstand seats could be had for £1, enclosure tickets would set you back 5/– (25p in current values) and for those prepared to take their chance in the elements and stand behind the posts the cost was 3/– (15p).

If ever an international rugby match should not have been

played it was that between Wales and England in January 1963. The pitch may have benefited from its covering of straw but the two teams remained in the changing rooms during the playing of the national anthems because it was too cold to stand around for those few emotional minutes. The Welsh players were issued with a layer of underwear and mittens to help stave off the desperate cold and captain Clive Rowlands likened the sound of the players' studs as they eventually ran out, to that of cattle on a tarmac surface – click, click, click. When England won the match 13–6 much thought must have been given as to why it had been allowed to take place.

As early as 10 January the WRU had announced an extension to the current season. Tradition dictated that rugby football was only to be played between 1 September and 30 April, but with so many fixtures lost to the weather and club treasurers reaching for the bottle, the Union gave dispensation for matches to be rearranged. Clubs were given an extra week to try and boost the coffers, seven days in which to accommodate some of the outstanding fixtures. A decision that would have helped some clubs but, as the season drew to a close, Newport did not need the seven-day window to tie up any loose ends.

The club had seen nine matches called off as a direct result of the extreme weather. The Royal Navy and Oxford University would not now visit Rodney Parade, neither would Newport travel to the Watsonians, Coventry, or Leicester, but room was found in the already congested months of March and April to entertain Llanelli, Ebbw Vale and Cardiff and travel to Swansea. It was a match at Cardiff that would breathe life back into the season, which for Newport began again on Saturday, 2 March. It was going to be a busy couple of months.

Like all others, the 1962–3 season welcomed some new faces to Rodney Parade and witnessed the departure of a few familiar ones. Among those drafted in and who would eventually become regular first-team players were outside-half or centre Eddie Mogford, prop Brian Perrins and number eight John Mantle. The highest profile departure was that of Norman

Morgan. The full-back joined the club in 1955 but a bad knee injury sustained against the Watsonians on Boxing Day 1960 kept him out of the game for twelve months. Morgan played the second half of the 1961–2 season and began the next with all good intent but after nine appearances, he decided it was time to call it a day. During Morgan's prolonged absence Newport had secured the services of Barry Edwards from Tredegar and after a baptism of fire against the touring Springboks, Edwards had settled into the role of first-choice full-back. With Morgan's departure confirmed, the club realised there was no back-up for Edwards and the first priority on the resumption of fixtures in March was to find a player who could fill the role.

Ray Cheney joined Pontypool in 1955. By the 1960s he was considered to be among the best full-backs in Wales. A regular Welsh reserve, Cheney was unable to break into the team due to the presence of firstly Llanelli's Terry Davies and Newport's Norman Morgan and more recently Kelvin Coslett from Aberavon and Neath's Grahame Hodgson. When Coslett signed professional papers with St Helens RLFC in 1962, Cheney could see himself getting ever closer to international honours but perhaps he was playing at the wrong club.

Future Welsh captain Clive Rowlands had recently arrived at Pontypool and introduced a system which saw Cheney's role, as the last line of defence, move away from the normal pattern. As an accurate kicker of the ball out of hand, scrum-half Rowlands liked to work the touchlines and took upon himself the responsibility of marshalling the defence out wide, preferring his full-back to operate in midfield. This may have worked at club level but Cheney felt it would do his international prospects no good if he was seen to be remaining in the middle of the field of play for much of the time. This was confirmed when Welsh selector, Rees Stephens, had a quiet word with him. Clearly Rowlands' tactical approach to the game detracted from traditional full-back play and perhaps Cheney would enhance his chances of playing for Wales if he looked for another club. Pontypool would not change their style of play to accommodate one player's personal interests but it was recently retired prop Ray Prosser who pointed the full-back in the direction of either Cardiff or Newport. Alan Priday was the full back in residence at the Arms Park but things looked more promising at Rodney Parade where Norman Morgan had announced his retirement. Throw into the equation that Cheney was working in Newport at the time and was good friends with hooker Graham Bevan, then a move to Newport RFC became the obvious choice.

So who was the mystery player about to make his debut at Rodney Parade? The *South Wales Argus* got some mileage out of the fact that a new player of some standing was about to join Newport, but no name was mentioned until very late in the day. Certain protocols had to be observed when a player changed clubs, particularly in mid-season, and it was Edwards who played at Cardiff and against the Wasps, but in the first home match following the resumption of club rugby after the bad winter, Ray Cheney became a Newport player, making his debut against Llanelli at Rodney Parade in one of the rearranged fixtures.

He quickly established himself as first-choice full-back, playing in eleven of the remaining 15 matches and scoring 40 points with six penalties and eleven conversions. Cheney would continue to rack up the points with the boot in the coming seasons, breaking Morgan's club record at the first attempt in 1963–4 and then improving on it next time round when he became the first Newport player to score over 200 points in a season, registering 224, made up of 73 conversions and 26 penalty goals. That was all a bit further down the road but for anyone casting a watchful eye over the playing squad assembled at Rodney Parade as the interrupted season moved toward its conclusion, it is certain they would not have realised that 13 pieces of a small but nevertheless fascinating jigsaw were now in place.

Having experienced such a woeful first four months of the season, Newport looked a much improved side when fixtures resumed. Seventeen matches were somehow shoehorned into

March and April, played over 52 days in fact, with only the away trips to Gloucester and Swansea ending in defeat. Cardiff shared an 8–8 draw at Rodney Parade but Aberavon, Neath, Bridgend, Ebbw Vale and the Barbarians were among the clubs who found the revitalised Black and Ambers too strong. This successful run ensured that what had earlier looked likely to go on record as one of the club's less distinguished campaigns could be viewed in a much better light. Newport ended the season with 26 of the 42 matches played won, with three drawn. The breakdown of results before the weather took control show twelve wins and two draws among the 25 results, thereby confirming what was a significant improvement – Newport RFC was on a roll!

While Britain was covered in a blanket of white, 12,000 miles away in a land where black is the favoured colour, final details were being completed for a major tour which New Zealand would undertake later in the year. Between October and the following February, the All Blacks would play a total of 36 matches: 30 in Britain and Ireland, four in France, and two in Canada on the way home. Such tours were a massive undertaking and, in the days when the game was strictly amateur, it asked a lot of those players selected. The party would be away from New Zealand for the best part of five months, through a northern hemisphere winter to boot and when the climate they would leave behind would be at its best. Reports of the extreme winter recently experienced in Britain would have certainly reached New Zealand, but such inconveniences would not be allowed to stand in the way of the All Blacks if there was to be a repeat of the extreme conditions in twelve months time.

When the full itinerary was confirmed on 15 January it showed that nine matches were scheduled to take place in Wales. New Zealand would play Wales in Cardiff on 21 December and the finale against the star-studded Barbarians was also due to be played at Cardiff Arms Park on 15 February. Elsewhere on the fixture list three combination sides would have to put local rivalries aside, try to plot the tourists' downfall and claim a famous scalp. Aberavon & Neath at Talbot Athletic Ground, Port Talbot; Abertillery & Ebbw Vale at Abertillery Park; together with Pontypool & Cross Keys at Pontypool Park. They were all expected to play in front of full houses. But it was the four matches against stand-alone Welsh clubs that would generate the greatest expectation of success. Cardiff, Llanelli, Newport and Swansea were granted the high-profile fixtures and Newport would have first crack at the tourists when they arrived at Rodney Parade on Wednesday, 30 October for what would be the third match of the tour. But who were these All Blacks? New Zealand had last toured Britain ten years earlier. Since then, only newspaper reports of the 1959 British Lions tour had kept rugby followers abreast of what was happening in the Antipodes. So, who exactly were these men in black?

CHAPTER TWO

A Land of Giants

"Ladies and gentlemen, we are about to begin our descent to Auckland. Please return your seats to the upright position, make sure all cigarettes are extinguished and that your seat belts are securely fastened... And put your watches back 50 years..."

Source unknown

NEW ZEALAND OFFICIALLY entered the international rugby arena with an emphatic 22–3 victory against Australia, in a game held at Sydney Cricket Ground on 15 August 1903. As far back as 1884 matches had been played against both New South Wales and Queensland but neither opponent had the standing of an international team. Therefore, it is from 1903 onwards that we can compile the statistical information that reveals the highs and lows of New Zealand's impact on rugby union. The figures make sobering reading, as they reveal that not only has New Zealand contested international rugby matches against all the leading rugby playing nations for over a century, but has dominated the game – most of the time.

A statistical overview of world rugby taken in 2013 shows that New Zealand has a positive record against all international opponents, the only country able to make such a boast. South Africa comes closest to threatening the overall supremacy of their great rivals, but still trail by 14 in the series of matches played between the two countries. Australia's 41 victories over their near neighbours is somewhat surprising, until one considers that the Wallabies have been on the receiving end on no less than 99 occasions. The close proximity of these two great rugby-playing nations accounts for the number of matches played, but meetings between the All Blacks and the northern hemisphere countries are considerably fewer in number. Neither Ireland or Scotland has registered a victory from the 27 and 29 matches played respectively. Desperately poor returns and in marked contrast to France, which can lay claim to twelve victories against the men in black. England may or may not be content with having defeated New Zealand seven times from 35 meetings but spare a thought for Wales. Following the first four encounters between the two countries, Wales were leading the series 3–1. That was in 1953 since when a further 25 matches have taken place with New Zealand winning the lot. Maybe it is best to take the advice of the man on the flight deck and put the watch back those 50 years.

By 1963 the four home countries, under the guise of firstly the British Isles then the British Lions, had visited New Zealand six times, most recently in 1959 when a Test series that courted much controversy ended with a 3–1 win for the home side. England would visit New Zealand in the summer of 1963, the first of the home nations to do so, but that aside, the only opportunities England, Ireland, Scotland or Wales had to test their respective strengths and qualities against the All Blacks came when New Zealand embarked on a major tour to the northern hemisphere. The team scheduled to visit Britain, Ireland, France and North America through the winter of 1962–3 would be the fifth to undertake such a venture and their predecessors had set down a high benchmark for them to try to emulate.

It all started as far back as 1905, when a squad of 27 players under the captaincy of Dave Gallaher kicked off a 36-match tour against Devon at Exeter on 16 September. It would be almost five months before the final match of an exhausting enterprise took place in San Francisco on 13 February 1906. Throw in the best part of another ten weeks travelling, and the time spent away from home was almost seven months. All but one of the matches were won, the only defeat came at the hands of Wales in a match played at Cardiff Arms Park on 16 December, the home team winning the closest of encounters 3–0, a try by right wing Teddy Morgan separating the sides at the final whistle. This match is as much remembered for the try that wasn't as it is for Morgan's winning effort. Centre three-quarter Bob Deans appeared to have tied the scores when he grounded the ball over the Welsh goal line but Scottish referee, J.D. Dallas, was behind play and hadn't seen the touch-down. When he caught up the ball was lying six inches short of the line and on that evidence he disallowed the score. Had Welsh scrum-half Dicky Owens done the unthinkable and repositioned the ball as the New Zealand players were celebrating? Truth is we will never know but the incident is still a major topic of conversation whenever the two countries meet.

With much of Europe in turmoil following the outbreak of World War I it was almost 20 years before the second New Zealand tourists left home on what would be another mammoth expedition. These All Blacks would play four fewer matches than their predecessors but there was a case of déjà vu when the tour got under way on 13 September against Devon, albeit at a change of venue, the match taking place at the Rectory Ground in Devonport. Was this the greatest New Zealand team? Certainly the results suggest Cliff Porter's men were an exceptional group winning all 32 games played, most of them with seemingly ridiculous ease. But there was one encounter which saw the tourists on the back foot for much of the time and trailing on the scoreboard as the game entered the final minutes. That had been at Rodney Parade and the home side could only look on and wonder what might have been as a missed kick to touch saw New Zealand launch a counterattack which led to a try by 'Snowy' Svenson which Mark Nicholls converted to establish a 13–10 lead and the game was lost. After dominating every aspect of play, Newport had somehow managed to snatch defeat from the jaws of victory. In 1905 the Black and Ambers had contested a tight encounter before going down 6–3 to what was the better side on the day, but in 1924 a golden opportunity to become the only team to defeat the tourists slipped away.

Eleven years later the third All Blacks arrived for a tour now reduced to 30 matches but which saw the Welsh share of the fixtures increased to eight. Wales, Cardiff, Llanelli, Newport and Swansea were included once more with the pairings of Abertillery & Cross Keys and Aberavon & Neath introduced for the first time. In a gesture that raised many an eyebrow, the WRU awarded the final fixture within its discretion to a combination team labelled Mid-District. Made up of players from junior clubs, the scratch team would meet the tourists at Ynys Park, Aberdare in the Rhondda Valley.

When Swansea claimed a famous victory in the fifth match of the tour, the incredibly high standards seen in 1924–5 were firmly consigned to the record books, forgotten in an instant and word soon spread throughout the principality that these All Blacks were beatable. All of which looked a tad optimistic when, in the last ten days of October Llanelli, Cardiff and finally Newport were all comfortably defeated, the latter going down by 17 points to five. The All Blacks continued their winning ways through England and Scotland before the men of Ulster held the tourists to a 3–3 draw to once again lift the hopes of teams still to play them on their return to Wales.

Comfortable victories against Mid-District and Aberavon & Neath brought the optimists back to earth and now all roads led to Cardiff for the much anticipated meeting with Wales. The game would be recognised as the best of the tour. A fine game of rugby which led New Zealand captain Jack Manchester to remark, "it did not matter who won it". Wales ran out eventual winners by 13 points to twelve and when England scored a first victory against New Zealand two weeks later the record of these third All Blacks looked more than slightly tarnished – played 30, won 26, drew one, lost three. Was the balance of power shifting?

Just as the outbreak of World War I meant that there was a 20-year gap between the first and second New Zealand tours, now World War II impacted in similar fashion, and it would be another 18 years before the fourth All Blacks arrived in Britain. The introduction of long haul air travel meant the time spent in transit was much reduced, but Bob Stuart's team faced an expanded itinerary that saw 36 fixtures back on the schedule. Much of March would be spent in North America, where five games were due to be played, while in Britain the WRU was once more disposed to allocate seven matches in addition to the international that would be played on 19 December. Gone was the Mid-District fixture, replaced by another combined team which saw Abertillery now paired with Ebbw Vale, and Pontypool brought into the mix to join forces with Cross Keys. Elsewhere it was the same again, Neath joining forces with Aberavon and Cardiff, Llanelli, Newport and Swansea the only clubs granted stand-alone status, much to the chagrin of all others both within and beyond the Welsh border.

The tourists coasted through the first six matches with comparative ease before arriving in Cardiff to play a team that was without doubt the best club side in Britain at the time. Realising the threat to their record, New Zealand fielded the strongest side to date, and would not claim to have been inconvenienced by the late withdrawal of captain Bob Stuart. Cardiff rose to the occasion magnificently and ran out 8–3 winners, emulating Swansea's triumph in 1935. Not to be out done, the west Wales club responded in fine style three weeks later, holding the tourists to a 6–6 draw. Seven days on and it was the turn of Wales to steal the All Blacks' thunder by recording a third victory over New Zealand and take that 3–1 lead in the matches played between the two countries.

Into the new year and once again the men of Ulster proved equal to the task, contesting another drawn match. From Ireland the tourists returned to Wales for three matches, among them an encounter with Newport at Rodney Parade. Desperate to emulate Cardiff and Swansea, the Black and Ambers were once again found wanting, this time going down 11–6 in another frustratingly close match. As the tour drew to the conclusion of its European leg, firstly South-West France in Bordeaux and three days later France in Paris, both defeated the All Blacks and Bob Stuart's team were sent home with the worst record of the four New Zealand touring teams to venture north – played 36, won 30, two drawn with four defeats – two in Wales and two in France.

Looking at the four tours collectively, the figures show that of the 134 matches played, 123 were won, two drawn and eight lost. Five of the defeats had been in internationals, with Wales claiming three victories, England and France one apiece. Cardiff and Swansea, together with South-West France made up the rest. Not a poor return by any reckoning, but more was demanded by the followers of the game back home and much would be expected of the next group of men to pull on the black jersey in northern climes.

When New Zealand left these shores in March 1954 it really could have been a case of, out of sight, out of mind. Technology had a long way to go before the major matches played around the world could be enjoyed in the comfort of one's home, transmitted live through the medium of television. Certainly, rugby carried on in the southern hemisphere, Australia, New Zealand and South Africa knocking lumps out of each other at every opportunity but, other than the score possibly being noted in broadsheets such as *The Times* it is unlikely that any further information would be forthcoming. That New Zealand won a home series against South Africa in 1956 and that the Springboks got their revenge when the All Blacks visited South Africa four years later was of little consequence to rugby supporters whose main interest in international rugby was satisfied by the Five Nations Championship. France's first tour of New Zealand in 1961 may well have received more coverage, but one suspects that this would not have gone beyond the Test series which the French lost 3–0. The All Blacks played two Tests in Australia in 1957 and the following year the Wallabies played a three-Test series in New Zealand but, until the British Lions toured in 1959, for followers of the game north of the Equator, the All Blacks might just as well have been playing their rugby on another planet.

The British media took the Lions tour seriously and there was ample coverage in the press to satisfy a rugby public eager to keep up to date with the fortunes of the tourists. Such was the interest that come Christmas there would be books published detailing the on- and off-the-field events down under. What they would also confirm is that the Lions played some fine rugby, won the hearts of the home supporters, were great ambassadors off the field but lost the Test series 3–1. Much has been written about the infamous first Test which the All Blacks stole 18–17; six penalty goals from the boot of full-back Don Clarke denying a superior Lions team that ran in four thrilling tries. Clarke was the younger brother of prop forward Ian who had toured Britain with the All Blacks in 1953/54, while packing down on the other side of the front row was the New Zealand captain, Wilson Whineray. Between them, hooker Ron Hemi was another throwback to the fourth All Blacks, but elsewhere there were faces and names largely unfamiliar to any Lion who had played against New Zealand six years earlier. Among those players introduced to Test rugby against the Lions were Kel Tremain at wing forward, scrum-half Kevin Briscoe and left wing Ralph Caulton, who bagged a brace of tries when making his debut in the second Test and ran in two more in the third. Of the three-quarters Pat Walsh had previous Test match experience, as had Colin Meads who featured at both wing forward and in the second row against the tourists.

Representing Newport RFC on the tour were centre Malcolm Thomas and hooker Bryn Meredith. Thomas was the first player to visit New Zealand with two British Lions parties, having toured in 1950 when he won two caps on the wing. Now he would only make one Test appearance, but it was one more than Meredith, who was forced to watch on from the stands – tour captain Ronnie Dawson claiming the hooking duties in the Test series. Bryn Meredith toured South Africa with the Lions in 1955, where he played a starring role winning four caps and he would go on to repeat the feat in 1962 when the Lions returned to that country. But, in 1959 he had to play second fiddle to the tour captain. Meredith was widely recognised as the superior player, but this counted for nothing when it came to team selection for the Tests, an embarrassing scenario which is avoided when looking for a Lions captain today – the player chosen has to be first choice in his given position.

From his privileged seat in the grandstand, Meredith saw Don Clarke kick goals from all over the park, the fleet of foot Ralph Caulton run in four tries, Wilson Whineray lead his team from the front with great aplomb and tactical awareness, and the power house that was Colin Meads could not be missed whichever position he filled neither could the barnstorming play of Kel Tremain. Together with Ian Clarke and Kevin Briscoe, here were seven players who each made a significant contribution to New Zealand rugby during their careers, seven players who four years later would take to the field 12,000 miles away at a Welsh club ground on a wet Wednesday afternoon.

The domestic rugby season in New Zealand once ran from the beginning of May through to the end of September. Times have changed but, in 1962, the last round of provincial matches was played on 29 September after which the players could look forward to a long summer away from the demands of the union game, with the pre-season trials scheduled for early May. The New Zealand Rugby Football Union may have had other ideas when announcing a 71-man squad comprising of 33 backs and 38 forwards who were to keep training throughout the summer months in preparation for an extended season. This would begin with a short tour by Queensland, quickly followed by England's five-match itinerary which included two Tests. With the All Blacks due to leave for Britain in early October there would be no respite, particularly for those players selected to tour at the end of the season. Keep in training through the summer? Train on your own? Yes and yes again – that was what was expected of those with aspirations of wearing the silver fern in 1963.

Long before a bearded, long-haired film director by the name of Peter Jackson carved out great swathes of New Zealand, claimed it as his own, and populated it with all manner of fantastic individuals and creatures. Long before Bilbo Baggins set off on his incredible adventure and Gandalf weaved his magical powers. Long before those aficionados of J.R.R. Tolkien, Middle-earth, *The Hobbit* and *Lord of the Rings* packed their rucksacks and set off in their thousands for Jackson's corner of New Zealand to trek the paths well worn by Tolkien's creations. Long before all of that, legend has it that in the 1950s, 1960s and even into the 1970s, there were several reported sightings in and around King Country on the west coast of New Zealand's North Island, of a giant of a man running up hills and down dale with a fully-grown sheep under each arm. Locals came to call him Pinetree, and he would later be acclaimed as New Zealand's greatest rugby player of the 20th century. Standing 6' 4" tall and weighing in at 15 stone 12 pounds, his name was Colin Earl Meads and he farmed the land, an occupation that demanded a high level of personal fitness, running around collecting stray sheep and carrying them back to wherever sheep are meant to be. Meads didn't need any directive from the New Zealand RFU regarding extra-curricular training, he was the finished article and lookout anybody who got in his way on a rugby field.

Mighty individual that he was, Meads had to stand up and be counted like all the other hopefuls who joined him in the trials held at the beginning of May. The process of elimination and final selection saw the team to face England at Eden Park, Auckland include some well-established players who had faced the 1959 Lions. Wilson Whineray was still captain, the Clarke brothers were both selected, as were Caulton, Tremain and Meads. The six would feature in both Tests against England and each looked certain to be invited to tour Britain later in the year. For Don and Ian Clarke the second Test would have special significance as it would see each brother win his 24th cap, a New Zealand record.

England were well beaten in Auckland but the match the following week was a much more closely contested encounter, the score standing at 6–6 with five minutes to play. Many laws of the game have long since been dispensed with, among them the opportunity to kick for goal from what was termed a fair catch. A player catching the ball in open play and calling a mark could then opt to kick for goal from a point behind where the catch was claimed, allowing the opposition to stand on the mark from which they were allowed to charge when the goal kicker commenced his run up. When Don Clarke claimed a fair catch and elected to kick for goal, the England forwards were deemed to have charged too soon and a penalty was awarded allowing Clarke a kick at goal which could not be charged. It is doubtful if this passage of play has ever been missed following its revision in the laws of the game, but for England that came too late. Don Clarke converted the winning goal from what is reported as being 65 yards which certainly gave the visitors something to mull over on the long flight home – here was a player who was capable of punishing any indiscretions from the halfway line and beyond.

Followers of the game in New Zealand, which should probably read *all* of New Zealand, were hoping for great things from the All Blacks on the forthcoming tour. That there was an accompanying degree of pessimism not normally associated with wearers of the silver fern was something of a surprise.

If the tourists could complete the tour with three or four defeats on the log, then they would be seen to have done well. Why such negativity? This couldn't be playing mind games, as such nonsense was yet to be invented. No, the lack of optimism can be traced back to that day in May at Lancaster Park, Christchurch when the All Blacks got out of jail against England courtesy of a mighty kick from the boot of Don Clarke and all who witnessed the match knew it. England had rattled the home team, were the better side on the day and deserved at the very least to draw the match.

When the names of the 30 players selected to tour were announced in September, it did little to convince the party poopers that they might have prejudged the situation, that this was a group of players ready to emulate the 1905 and 1924 vintages. The general consensus was that if the fifth All Blacks did as well as their immediate predecessors who lost four and drew two matches, they would be allowed back into the country. Anything less would herald an extended period of mourning. What was the problem? Time would prove there wasn't one, but as is always the case when it comes to putting forward names on a sheet of paper opinions differ as to who should be included and who should be ignored. Best left to those who know best and in 1963 they appear to have managed their task well.

The party was made up of 20 players from North Island and ten from South Island. That imbalance would not have gone down well in Canterbury and Otago despite Canterbury having most representatives with six. The forwards were considered big for sure, averaging a little over 15 stone per man which was half a stone more than their counterparts in Bob Stuart's team. With an average height of 6' 1" the pack was going to take some holding in the tight and the players' mobility was never going to be in doubt. With only four uncapped players among them, there was a wealth of experience up front to draw on and it would take a mighty effort from an opposing eight to get the better of that lot.

The party would be led by Wilson Whineray. The Auckland prop first captained New Zealand in 1958, since when he had led the team in 21 consecutive Tests. Joining him in the front row was Ian Clarke who had toured with the fourth All Blacks ten years earlier, together with two less experienced props, Jules le Lievre and Ken Gray, the latter destined to become one of New Zealand's best tight forwards for many generations. The hooking duties would be shared by Dennis Young, at 33 the oldest tourist with 17 caps to his name and the uncapped John Major.

Four second-row forwards were selected. Colin Meads was joined by his younger brother Stan, together with Alan Stewart and Ron Horsley, all of whom had played Test rugby. Of the six loose forwards Kel Tremain, Kevin Barry, Keith Nelson and the uncapped Brian Lochore could each play in the second row if required. John Graham and Waka Nathan would contest the open-side wing forward position with the experienced Graham more than comfortable in all three back row positions.

Among their number the All Blacks boasted the most prolific points scoring machine rugby football had ever seen. Not only was Don Clarke consistently accurate with his place kicking, but his range was extraordinary and any penalties awarded within 60 yards of goal would likely be punished to the tune of three points a time. Clarke was a big man. At 16 stone 9 pounds he was the heaviest tourist and his 6' 2" was only improved on by the four lock forwards. This man mountain was also surprisingly quick, but like all things big, going forward or backwards in a relatively straight line was fine, but turning around was another matter. This took time, more time than might be at his disposal if he came up against some clever half-backs who could drop a rugby ball on a sixpence. And like all players, Clarke might get injured. Where would the selectors look then?

Don Clarke had only missed one Test since his debut in 1956. Injury had forced him out of contention and his place was taken by Lloyd Ashby, the Southland full-back who would win his only cap in a 6–3 defeat by Australia. Prior to Clarke's introduction, Pat Walsh was full-back, but that had been seven years earlier and although Walsh was included in the tour party it was as a centre, but he would be one option to consider when Clarke needed a rest. Another was the young Maori first five-eighth, Mac Herewini, who was also a competent goal kicker. Good alternatives maybe, but there was little doubt that if Clarke was indisposed he would be sorely missed. So you have a no nonsense pack that will take some controlling and a full-back who could apparently kick goals from all bar the most remote areas of the pitch – what about the rest of the backs?

Three of the four selected wing three-quarters were uncapped. Malcolm Dick, Bill Davis and Ian Smith, together with seasoned Test player Ralph Caulton, would hope to see enough of the ball to rattle up the tries, something which would be totally dependant on the men inside them. In New Zealand rugby parlance, an outside-half is a first five-eighth, an inside-centre a second five-eighth and an outside-centre – well he is a centre. On this basis the uncapped Ian MacRae and Auckland's Paul Little would be expected to share duties on the outside of the midfield with the back-in-favour Pat Walsh and Derek Arnold each hoping to get the nod from the selectors at second five-eighth when the time came to sit down and choose the Test team. As the tour unfolded, so would the eight three-quarters each prove themselves adaptable enough to mix and match at the selectors' whim.

The five nominated half-backs could boast only ten international appearances between them. Of the three first five-eighths, Bruce Watt was the more experienced with four caps, Mac Herewini had one and Earl Kirton, one of the surprise selections, was yet to play Test rugby. His scrum-half partner at Otago was also uncapped but much was expected of Chris Laidlaw, who would be vying for pole position with the five times capped Kevin Briscoe who was also appointed tour vice-captain. Did this apparent lack of experience in two of the most critical positions on the field suggest an area where New

Zealand could be vulnerable? Time would tell, and it would be down to tour manager Frank Kilby and his assistant Neil McPhail, together with the captain, to make those important selection decisions.

Kilby had represented New Zealand between 1928–34, the first five-eighth captaining the side four times. Originally from Southland, Kilby had experience as a selector for Auckland and had also managed the New Zealand Maoris on a tour of Australia in 1958. The war years had almost certainly come between Neil McPhail and a New Zealand cap, but he gained some consolation when touring Britain with the Kiwi Army team in 1945–6. Previously a selector with Canterbury, McPhail was the current chairman of the New Zealand selectors.

Thirty players and two managers. Among their number were eight farmers, with four other players employed in businesses directly associated with agriculture. Eight worked in commerce and there were two schoolteachers, two students, two were involved in the oil industry and one in construction. Perhaps the most useful of their number were Keith Nelson, a dentist who may or may not have taken the tools of his trade with him; Don Clarke, a cigarette salesman who may or may not have had the necessary contacts in Britain to generate a supply of tobacco for the puffers in the party; and Paul Little, a hairdresser who would surely have been expected to keep the players looking trim and dapper up top, free of charge. Manager, Frank Kilby was a bank manager, and assistant manager Neil McPhail a company director, which would ensure that the small weekly stipend received by the players and all other incidental expenses would be accurately recorded for the New Zealand RFU's auditors, the major costs of the tour underwritten by the four home Unions.

On 11 October the players and management met as a group for the first time in Wellington, having arrived from departure points across the length and breadth of the land. With six players in the party Canterbury topped the list of representatives, closely followed by Auckland with five and four from Otago. Three players came from Hawke's Bay with four provinces providing two; Taranaki and Wellington, with Waikato represented by the Clarke brothers and the Meads siblings from King Country. The numbers were made up by a player from each of Counties, Wairarapa, Thames Valley and Manawatu.

Two days later the party set off on the long flight north, arriving in London on 16 October. Once there they enjoyed a week in which to acclimatise, get over any jet lag and blow the cobwebs away before the opening match of the tour which took place on 23 October at Iffley Road, Oxford against the students of the famous university. Both Oxford University and the equally lauded seat of learning that is Cambridge University had enjoyed fixtures against the four previous New Zealand touring sides and it would be no different this time, Cambridge due to meet the All Blacks in November.

Iffley Road played host to 12,000 spectators on that autumn afternoon. Among the number were four men who were on a spying mission. They had set off by road early that morning on the 100-mile journey which took them to Gloucester via the A48 where they connected with the A40 for the scenic route through the Cotswolds and on to their final destination. They watched the afternoon's proceedings with interest. Notes were made on the individual players, the tactics, the strengths and any perceived weaknesses in the armoury. These would all be discussed in depth over the next week because in seven days time it would be the turn of Newport RFC to play host to the All Blacks, and there was much work to be done before then.

CHAPTER THREE

Looking for a Team

"A hard man is good to find."

Mae West (1892–1980)

THE SEVEN-DAY EXTENSION to the season granted by the WRU ended on 7 May, and with spring heading into summer rugby was soon forgotten. Trial matches aside, no rugby would be played before 1 September. After eight months during which many players appeared in excess of 40 matches, some as many as 50, the four-month break was always welcome. Rest assured, September would come soon enough but before then May, June, July and August had to be negotiated and in 1963 there was no shortage of distractions to help them along their way.

There were holidays to be taken, a one- or two-week break which most families would endeavour to spend at a popular seaside resort. Travelling by car from Newport, this could mean the short trip to Barry Island or a longer one further west to the Gower Peninsula. The more adventurous might cross the Bristol Channel, opting either for the long route via Gloucester or preferring to save on the miles and time by taking the ferry service that once operated between Beachley and Aust. Both options provided gateways to Devon and Cornwall, Torquay on the English Riviera and further along the south coast Weymouth and Bournemouth were perennial favourites.

For those with sufficiently deep pockets and looking to

broaden their horizons, local travel companies could arrange some tempting alternatives. Fly to Majorca? Who would have believed it, but this was one of the many destinations now within reach and a 15-day flight and hotel package would set you back 36 guineas with Pickfords Travel. Prefer the idea of a stay at one of the Costas or alpine walking in Austria? Sky Tours could provide the perfect package with transport by coach to Luton Airport from where a four-engine pressurized Constellation was waiting to whisk holidaymakers off for eleven and twelve-day breaks from £30 per person. And if you didn't own a car and the thought of taking to the airways failed to grab the imagination, then there was always the train – but you might need to be quick!

The disruption to the rail network caused during the exceptionally bad winter was as nothing compared to that soon to result from the Beeching Report – 'The Reshaping of British Railways', which was published in March. Debt ridden and losing vast sums of money, the railway system was a constant drain on the government purse and something had to be done. On the recommendation of Minister of Transport, Ernest Marples, Prime Minister Harold Macmillan appointed Dr Richard Beeching to the post of Chairman of the British Transport Commission, with the brief of carrying out an in-depth investigation into the operation of the railways and produce a comprehensive report together with recommendations. That the ICI director, whose background lay in accountancy, failed on a monumental scale continues to haunt the railway network 50 years on. Beeching's report focussed on where savings could be made and, over the next few years, more than 2,000 stations would be closed and in excess of 3,000 miles of track fell into disuse leading to many small provincial towns and villages being removed from the system. And still the railways failed to generate a profit.

When ill health forced Anthony Eden to resign from office in 1957, Harold Macmillan was elected leader of the Conservative party and with it came the keys to Number 10 Downing Street.

Macmillan's premiership was one of many highs and lows. He is well remembered for the 'wind of change' speech delivered in Cape Town in February 1960, in which he warned that political power should be determined regardless of race. His words went unheeded, and the Sharpeville massacre in March confirmed the worse fears of a nation on the brink. Twelve months later South Africa withdrew its membership of the Commonwealth and on 31 May 1961 it became a republic. More famously, shortly after taking office, Macmillan addressed a gathering in Bedford declaring that 'most of our people have never had it so good', another boat rocking exercise.

Understandably, less is written about Harold Macmillan's presence at Twickenham on 16 March 1963 when he was introduced to the England and Scotland teams before witnessing one of the great solo tries by an England player, that scored by outside-half and captain Richard Sharp, which helped secure the championship for the men in white. Neither does a passing comment made in July spring to mind when discussing the prime minister of the day. 'I was determined that no British government should be brought down by the action of two tarts...' were the words attributed to Macmillan, but what was he referring to?

John Profumo, the then Secretary of State for War and Member of Parliament for Stratford-upon-Avon, became embroiled in a scandal that rocked and shocked the nation. The Profumo Affair dominated the headlines throughout the summer months, introducing a cast of players who would become household names. Christine Keeler, Mandy Rice-Davies, Stephen Ward, Eugene Ivanov and Lord Astor, together with a number of supporting players, joined Profumo in an episode of lies, sexual intrigue and political foolhardiness that could never have been scripted. Who slept with whom? Who said what to whom? Was the nation's security threatened? All of which led to the disgraced minister's resignation on 17 June after having earlier staunchly denied any impropriety. Stephen Ward, a key player in the scandal, committed suicide while awaiting sentencing following his conviction for what was described as moral turpitude, having been charged under the Sexual Offences Act of 1956 with living off the immoral earnings of women and procuring. The Old Bailey was the focus of attention from 22 July, but on the last day of the month and what was scheduled to be the final day of the trial, Ward took a fatal overdose of barbiturates.

No sooner had the dust settled on the Profumo Affair than the next major news story was about to break. In the early hours of Thursday, 8 August, the Glasgow to London mail train was stopped by a gang of 16 villains who made off with in excess of £2.5 million, the raid completed in an estimated 46 minutes. Bridego Bridge and Leathersdale Farm would become landmarks on the criminologists' map but it was the names of Ronnie Biggs, Buster Edwards, Gordon Goody and Bruce Reynolds, among others, that would pass into folklore. Modern day Robin Hoods they were not, but there is something about the Great Train Robbery that still ignites public interest like few major crimes either before or since. The money stolen equates to something in the region of £45 million in today's currency, and over the past 50 years the major protagonists have been somewhat glamorized by a plethora of books and films.

While political scandal and a gang of outlaws dominated the headlines during a summer that saw temperatures soar in marked contrast to the winter depths reached in the earlier part of the year, those stalwarts who played out their unsung roles behind the scenes at Rodney Parade were going about their duties. Newport RFC came under the umbrella of Newport Athletic Club which included cricket, tennis and bowls among its various playing sections. Beyond the rugby stadium there was a cricket ground which was the home of Newport Cricket Club and where, on occasion, Glamorgan CCC played home matches. During the summer months the large area of lawn between the clubhouse and rugby pitch would become the home of the tennis section, with seven or eight courts available to members. Before tennis became an open sport, the week immediately following Wimbledon saw the leading players head for either the Irish Championships held in Dublin or the Welsh Championships which took place at Rodney Parade.

Such a facility did not run itself and among the full-time staff employed were administrators who ran the day-to-day affairs of the general office, a steward who was responsible for the clubhouse facilities and the ground staff who were headed by Fred Cox. These were employees of Newport Athletic Club but it was the remit of each section to appoint its own committees and run its own affairs.

The workload generated by the rugby section, in particular, was time-consuming and but for the dedication of men committed to the task, it is difficult to imagine the club functioning. Bill Everson was honorary secretary of Newport RFC in 1963, ably abetted by Nick Carter, whose main function was that of honorary match secretary. When Carter finalised the details, and the fixture list for the coming season was published, it confirmed that in the first four months 25 matches would be played and that, come the end of April, the total would stand at 48, the highest number in a season since the club's formation in 1875. With such an extensive agenda to fulfil, the demands on players would be high. The final reckoning would show that 47 players appeared for Newport during the season. For many the number of appearances would be restricted to single figures, ten of them only playing in one match, while at the other end of the table were six players who had each been at the club long enough for the grandiose title of 'senior' to be attributed to them.

Second-row forward Brian Price was captain-elect for the coming season and it would not have passed the new leader's attention that when the All Blacks arrived at Rodney Parade on 30 October, he would be celebrating his 26th birthday. Price played four matches for the club in 1959–60, his final year at St Luke's College, but come the following season he had relocated to south Wales and his ready availability saw him make 36 appearances in a Newport jersey. It was during that 1960–1 season that Price was first capped and, after playing in Newport's narrow 3–0 defeat by the Springboks, he represented the Barbarians when the famous club became the only team to beat the tourists in the final match of the tour.

Price succeeded back-row forward Glyn Davidge as Newport captain. Newport born, Davidge joined the club in 1952 and would spend the next 13 seasons at Rodney Parade, playing in 270 matches. There were nine Welsh caps and a call-up as a replacement for Alun Pask on the 1962 British Lions tour to South Africa. Pask was injured in the third Test, but Davidge only made three appearances for the Lions before suffering a slipped disc which saw him sidelined for the first few months of the new season.

In its hour of need Newport turned to experienced centre Brian Jones to take over the captaincy duties, a role he was familiar with having led the club in the 1959–60 and 1960–1 seasons. Jones joined Newport in 1953 and in his first season with the club, the 18 year old featured in 18 matches, among them the 11–6 defeat by the fourth All Blacks. Ten years on, Brian Jones would be the sole survivor of that Newport team when the two sides met again. Much would happen between those two landmark matches, including a tour to South Africa with the Barbarians in 1958, two Welsh caps won in 1960 and Brian Jones joined Brian Price in the Barbarians team that defeated the Springboks in 1961.

Brian Price's partner in the second row for much of the 1960–1 season and beyond was a player well established at the club, having first played for Newport twelve years earlier. There was little to suggest what lay ahead when Ian Ford appeared in only one first-team match in his first season, and fared little better in the second, when he clocked up six. How things would change over the next 15 seasons, as his appearances in the Newport jersey gained momentum, until Ian Ford claimed the club record for the number of games played. Roy Burnett had featured in 372 matches for Newport but, come the end of the 1961–2 season, that record had been improved on by Ford, whose appearances now stood at 379. Ian Ford duly became the first Newport player to play 400 games for the club and, by the time he hung up his boots in 1966, he had extended his record to 482. Ford's mighty presence in the Newport second row was recognised in 1959 when he was selected to play for Wales against England and Scotland.

The foundation of any successful side has to start in the front row. The number of scrums contested in the modern game has reduced considerably but, in the 1960s, it was a major part of the contest and not to gain control up front invariably led to defeat. Prop Des Greenslade had decided to retire at the end of the 1962–3 season allowing David Jones the chance to make his mark in the team, make the tight-head position his own. He would join loose-head prop Neville Johnson and hooker Graham Bevan in forming a front row that was more than capable of holding its own in the set pieces. None of the trio would gain international honours but they were all admirable club men who unfailingly put their bodies on the line week-in week-out for the cause that was Newport rugby.

After making two appearances at the tail end of the 1959–60 season, Neville Johnson quickly established himself as a first-team player. He joined Bryn Meredith and Des Greenslade in a front row which he still considers not only the best he played in, but the best that ever represented the club. Unlike Meredith and Greenslade, the only international honours Johnson gained were playing for the Wales Under 15 and Wales Under 18 teams in the early 1950s. Wales would not send a representative side to the southern hemisphere until the tour to South Africa in 1964 but ten years earlier the Welsh Schoolboys visited the same country and, among the squad, was the 16-year-old Neville Johnson. Seven weeks away from home, two long sea journeys, courtesy of the Union Castle Line and rugby in a land where the people are as taken up with the game as they are in Wales.

On his return, Johnson began two years National Service with the RAF. Rugby continued by way of regular appearances for Bomber Command and the RAF, with the occasional guest appearance for London Welsh. His undoubted talent was spotted by Air Vice-Marshall Johnny Johnson, a committee member at the RFU, who invited him to take part in an English trial, an offer politely declined by the young Welshman who had other plans.

In 1958, with the regimen of National Service behind him, Johnson began a two-year course at St Luke's College, joining Brian Price who was now in his second year. Nev Johnson spent both years in the first team, during which time he also represented Devon in the English County Championship, before heading back to Wales to complete a year's teaching training course at Cardiff College of Education. As seen elsewhere, the college had first claim on its students and Johnson joined a team that included future Wales captain Clive Rowlands, and Dewi Bebb who would star on the left wing for Wales and the British Lions. Pontypridd RFC might have secured his services if not for an interest shown by Newport, and Neville Johnson would spend eight seasons at Rodney Parade before a back injury brought his career to a premature end. In the 1963–4 season, David Jones made 42 appearances, Graham Bevan 41 and Johnson played in 37 matches. That there were some doubts about the final make-up of the front row leading up to the game against New Zealand is somewhat surprising, but uncertainty there most surely was before the trio were finally given the green light.

Having been Bryn Meredith's understudy for five seasons, 1962–3 saw Graham Bevan finally get his chance of an extended run in the first team. He made the number two jersey his own, playing in 40 matches and come the start of the new season, it was unlikely that his place in the starting line-up would be threatened. One of the unsung heroes of the Newport team, Bevan would never attain international recognition but, during his nine seasons at Rodney Parade, he made the thick end of 200 appearances for the club, including 81 of the 90 matches played between 1962–4. Barring injury, here was one player guaranteed to take his place against the All Blacks, but who would support him in the scrums was open to debate.

As the opening day of the new season approached those closely involved with team selection would already have been weighing up the options available to them. In their minds the front row might still have been a work in progress, but any late thoughts on reshaping the balance would prove unnecessary. The Brian Price and Ian Ford partnership was unlikely to be broken and, with Algy Thomas and the four times capped Brian Cresswell either side of Davidge in the back row, the eight forwards likely to become first choice in their respective positions may well have been identified before the season was up and running, but they were not going to have things all their own way.

John Anderson would have certainly contested the blind-side position with Cresswell but for his departure at the end of the previous season. Over six campaigns Anderson scored 53 tries in 103 appearances for the club, but he signed for Huddersfield RLFC, adding his name to the long list of Welsh players to turn professional. Another back-row forward to have caught the eye was John Mantle. A student at Loughborough College, Mantle was limited to only two matches in the previous season, would play seven in 1963–4 and another 17 in 1964–5. Rarely has a player with so little game time made such a lasting impression at the club as did Mantle, a great prospect who would win two Welsh caps before following Anderson on the trek north when signing for St Helens RLFC in 1965. Rugby league would be the beneficiary of this player's great talent, Newport and Wales left to ponder on what might have been.

Hooker Vic Perrins was a home-grown product who joined

the club's youth team and would never leave Rodney Parade. Perrins proved a capable deputy for Bevan when called on and would later gain international honours winning two caps in 1970. In Bill Morris and David Husband, Newport had two second-row forwards to add much needed strength in depth to the boiler house. Morris was another Newport player destined to represent Wales. Prop forwards are perhaps the most enduring individuals in a rugby team and with David Jones and Neville Johnson unlikely to take a backward step, opportunities of playing for Newport in either of these positions were going to be scarce. The few crumbs available would be swooped on by Colin Prescott, but he was never going to get fat on such meagre offerings.

Behind the scrum the half-back positions looked to be secure in the capable hands of Bob Prosser and David Watkins, who were present in all but a handful of the matches played in the previous season. One of the centre positions would be taken by Brian Jones, but who would partner him was one of the unresolved issues the selectors would have to address with Eddie Mogford, Roddy Jones, Andy Morgan and Dick Uzzell all in contention. Mogford could deputise for David Watkins, if necessary, as indeed could Brian Jones, an all-round performer of the highest quality who was no stranger to the number ten jersey. Bob Prosser had an able deputy in Stuart Clode who would make nine appearances in the second half of the season but during 1963, it was Prosser who held court at scrum-half. During the year Newport played 42 matches, Prosser claiming the jersey in 39 of them with Pontypridd's Dennis John playing in the other three.

In recent seasons three players had dominated selection on the wing. Byron Thomas was the preferred choice on the right, with left wing specialists, Peter Rees and Dennis Perrott, sharing the duties on the other side of the field. When Thomas announced his intention to leave Rodney Parade for pastures new at Cardiff, the selectors were not slow in realising the huge gap this left. Finding a replacement who could slot in for the odd game was one thing, but the club did not have another proven exponent of the right wing position to call on. Thomas ran in 15 tries in what proved to be his final season with the club; he was a great favourite with the supporters and would prove difficult to replace. Leading the field was Alan Skirving who performed well in the trials and would be given an early opportunity to make his mark, playing in the first three games before injury brought the short run to an end, Skirving not returning to the team until 28 December.

The position of full-back, that all important last line of defence, would be contested between Ray Cheney and Barry Edwards who had earlier confirmed he would be staying at Rodney Parade. Both players were accomplished full-backs, both were competent goal kickers and both wanted to make the position his own – manna from heaven for any selector. To have two proven players vying for one position would surely bring out the very best in both, leaving the selection committee to watch on before making the all-important decision as to who should get the nod come the big game of the season.

It certainly appeared that if all things remained equal, there was a favourable following wind and if the leading players remained injury-free, then all the selectors had to concern themselves with when considering a match due to be played in two months' time was the make-up of the front row; who would join Brian Jones in the centre, who would replace Byron Thomas on the right wing and would Dennis Perrott or Peter Rees get the nod on the left. All of which appears pretty straightforward but, with twelve matches to play ahead of the club's big day, anything could happen.

Before Newport could begin to focus on the season proper, there was the usual round of trial matches to be played: opportunities for aspiring young players to show their skills, to try to convince those astute observers making notes in the grandstand that they had something to offer the famous club, that they had a dream to fulfil. Dreams were not exclusive to the next generation hoping to make its mark, they were equally important to the senior players who still wanted to be part of big days and, with one of the biggest not far off, they too were allowed to dream.

Dreams come in different packaging and in a variety of colours and, as the Newport players were preparing to take part in the trial matches that would see some ambitions realised and others shattered, on 28 August in Washington DC a leading figure in the civil rights movement was airing his dream to an audience of 250,000 and his words would reach across all of the western world. Standing in front of the Lincoln Memorial, Dr Martin Luther King addressed the gathering with a speech that reached way beyond Washington and the United States of America – 'I have a dream... I have a dream today.' Famous words that are representative of a struggle that took many years to win but one which eventually saw an African-American elected to the White House.

The only problem with Newport's opening fixture was that it was played at Rodney Parade. A trip to the Eternal City would have been a fine way to get the campaign up and running but that was never going to happen, such jollies way beyond the treasurer's purse. So it was that all roads led to Newport, with Rome represented by Roma Olympic, the city's leading rugby club about which less than next to nothing was known. Not much was known about Italian rugby full stop, but earlier in the year the national team had lost narrowly to France in a match played at Grenoble. With the minutes ticking away, the Italians were leading 12–6 but a late rally by the French secured the 14–12 victory. Before arriving at Newport, Roma had gone down to the Harlequins 14–16 and Swansea 0–12, results which suggested this would be no easy start to the season. And so it proved.

Aware of the outcome at the Stoop and St Helen's, the Newport selectors were not about to take any chances and Brian Price would lead a side that looked little short of the strongest available. Cheney, Alan Skirving making his debut, Brian Jones, Uzzell, Perrott, Watkins and Prosser lined up in the backs with David Jones, Bevan, Johnson, Price, Ford, Cresswell, Davidge and Thomas up front. Strange names were listed on the other side of the match day programme. The Roma captain was loose-head prop Levorato, with Perrinni, Amfranch, Romagnoli and Martini among those replacing the more familiar Jones, Williams and Davies. Before the game got under way the two captains were introduced on the field and, as is customary on such 'international' occasions, presentations were made. Brian Price gave the Roma captain a Newport pennant, in exchange he received a bunch of flowers, providing a humorous take on the formality for the press photographer to record for posterity.

The sun shone and there was some enterprising rugby from the visitors who looked like claiming a famous victory as the clock ran down, only for a late try by Dennis Perrott to level the scores at 8–8 and save Newport's blushes. Unfortunately, both Perrott and Cheney picked up injuries that saw them out of contention for the next five and six matches respectively. One game into the season and already two of the club's leading players were sidelined. Cheney's problem had been ongoing for a while and the time had come for it to be sorted. His left ankle was the issue and an X-ray confirmed he had a spur growing on the bone tissue and an operation was duly pencilled in for later in the month. This was carried out by Dr Nathan Rocyn Jones, a leading administrator in Welsh rugby and the man who would become President of the Welsh Rugby Union the following year.

At the start of each season the WRU would draw up a list of referees considered to be the best in the land and it was from this list that the men nominated to officiate the major club games would be chosen. Perform well and a referee could win a place on the international panel. The arrival of the All

Blacks would see more international rugby played during the season and the other fixtures on the itinerary would also demand the presence of the best referees. The men in the middle had a big part to play and there was much jostling for position when the time came for their number to be scrutinised with a view to who would be chosen to officiate in the choice fixtures.

In September the WRU nominated seven referees, with another two named as reserves. Each of the nominated referees would officiate one of the All Blacks club fixtures in Wales. F.G. Price from Blaenavon would be in charge when Aberavon & Neath played New Zealand, with Abertillery & Ebbw Vale enjoying the services of Gwillym J. Treharne, four days later. Llanelli's D.M. Hughes was given one of the plum fixtures when Cardiff took on the tourists at the Arms Park in front of what was expected to be a near capacity crowd, before it would be the turn of Pontypool & Cross Keys who would come under the jurisdiction of I. Matthews from Swansea. In the immediate build up to the Wales match, the All Blacks were scheduled to meet Swansea at St Helen's, where they would come under the watchful eye of Cwmavon's Meirion Joseph and Clydach's W. Thomas would be in charge when the tourists played their final club game in Wales against Llanelli. All of which meant that Newport and New Zealand would come under the watchful eye of Gwynne Walters from Gowerton, a small town located on the north of the Gower Peninsula in west Wales.

Gwynne Walters was one of the most recognisable referees on the rugby circuit, a familiar face at all the leading club grounds and it was Walters who had refereed Newport's opening match of the season against Roma. He would often take to the field wearing a cricket jersey and, although slight in stature, he would take to task the biggest of forwards when the need arose and there was never any doubting who was in charge. Gwynne Walters took to refereeing at an early age following a serious shoulder injury sustained in a road accident which brought any thoughts of playing senior rugby to an end. Walters was probably the youngest referee to pass the WRU's examination, so young in fact that he couldn't officiate senior matches for two years, until he reached what was once the landmark 21st birthday.

He began his career with the whistle in 1949, spending the next three seasons travelling the length and breadth of south Wales under the direction of the Union. Walters would often turn down the matches on offer and his first clash with officialdom came in June 1952 following a season in which it was calculated he had refused 16 of the 40 matches offered. These figures were unacceptable and he was told to improve on them or the WRU would be forced to dispense with his services. The following season saw Walters continue to be unavailable far too often, and matters were finally brought to a head when it was confirmed that he had been refereeing matches in England when his whistle was required in Wales. Letters from the WRU questioning his intentions went unanswered and the whole situation was getting out of hand. A further letter from the Union issued a stark warning – reply or his services would no longer be required.

Gwynne Walters finally responded. He had been captain of Gowerton Cricket Club in 1953 and as the season ran to the end of September, he was unavailable for refereeing duties for much of that month but yes, he had officiated at matches in England on 23 September, 17 October, 7 November and 9 January. The WRU, while appearing to accept the reasons offered, were far from satisfied and if Walters thought the matter had been laid to rest, he was wrong. As the season drew to a close, he received a letter from Eric Evans, Secretary of the WRU, informing him that his name had been removed from the list of official referees. The committee wished to express its thanks for services rendered etc., all of which gave the man who had looked like becoming one of rugby's finest referees much food for thought.

In December Gwynne Walters put pen to paper and wrote to the WRU regarding his removal from the list but he got short shrift, the Union only confirming that there was nothing to add. The position had arrived at an impasse from which it appeared there was no way forward. Walters had dedicated so much time to becoming a first-class referee and the WRU knew that here was a man whose services they needed. With the situation beginning to take on elements of farce, common sense finally prevailed when in February 1955 Gwynne Walters wrote to the WRU acknowledging there had been faults on his part and asking to be reinstated. The matter was finally resolved on 1 April and the following season the man in the cricket sweater was back on the circuit.

Walters was elected to the international panel of referees for the 1956-7 season, but it would be 1959 before he took control of his first international match, the meeting between France and Scotland held in Paris in January. The following year he officiated three Five Nations matches: England against Ireland at Twickenham, Ireland and Scotland in Dublin, and France versus England in Paris. Then in 1961 he was awarded France's fixture with the touring South Africans and a return to Paris for a game that was expected to produce more than the usual handbags at six paces scenario. For ten minutes it lived up to its billing but once Walters had laid down the law to the two captains, there was little doubt what would happen if matters continued to get out of hand. Walters' firm control won the day, confirming him as the leading referee in the northern hemisphere. The little man from Gowerton was where he had always wanted to be – at the top. More internationals, four Varsity matches and much else were on the CV come Gwynne Walters' selection to take control of Newport's match with New Zealand in October. It was Walters who officiated when Newport beat Australia 11-0 in 1957, and now he would return to officiate the club's biggest match of the new season. Highly respected by players and supporters alike, Gwynne Walters' appointment was well received by all concerned at Rodney Parade.

Two days after the Italian job, Monday night's home match against Penarth saw Colin Prescott, David Husband and John Mantle replace Neville Johnson, Ian Ford and Glyn Davidge up front, with Andy Evans, Peter Rees and Barry Edwards stepping in for Brian Jones, Dennis Perrott and Ray Cheney. Newport registered the expected victory by 23 points to nil, but at what cost? Now it was David Watkins who joined Perrott and Cheney on the injury list, the outside-half ruled out for the next six matches. Soon to join the trio was Alan Skirving, a nasty injury that caused some internal damage forcing him to leave the field at Bristol where Newport was comprehensively beaten 0–16, a result that could not be solely attributed to the club having to play much of the game reduced to 14 players. Only three matches into the season but already the committee were having to go about putting some contingency plans in place. The selectors knew that Watkins, Cheney and Perrott would return, given time, but were equally aware that Skirving would not be available for some months. Dennis Perrott had played on the right wing when required but he and Peter Rees were more at home on the left, and it would be sensible at this early stage of the season to resolve a problem that wasn't going to go away until a specialist was found to take up residence on the right hand side of the field.

Fully aware of the talent to be found at local clubs, the Newport selectors would have undoubtedly noted the try-scoring wing who was now in his fourth season at nearby Cross Keys. Stuart Watkins was born in Newport and educated at Caerleon where his skills with a ball saw him star for the school and local youth teams. He may have been showing signs of becoming a useful rugby player but his preferences lay elsewhere, in a sport where the ball was not elongated but of the round variety – Watkins eventually made a name for himself as a goal scoring centre-forward. A big rangy athlete with a long stride, Stuart Watkins had declined several offers from senior clubs inviting him to try his luck as a rugby player, but he finally gave in and took himself off to Cross Keys for a trial. When asked what position he played, he automatically replied centre-forward which saw him consigned to the wing where he was least likely to cause any serious disruption, after which he might just go away. He didn't. Stuart Watkins showed enough raw potential in the trial match to suggest that, given the right guidance and a copy of the laws of the game, he might just fit in.

It started badly when the new man dropped the first four passes he received in a senior rugby match. Send him packing was the opinion of some less than impressed spectators, but when he intercepted near his own line and ran the length of the field for an opportunist try, the doubters decided he might be worth a second chance. Over three seasons Watkins was given 136 chances to shine for the Keys, and he repaid this confidence by running in 70 tries. The player has long forgotten where the initial approach to join Newport came from, but it must have been in the first weeks of the new season because, on 21 September, he was included in the team that travelled to Neath where another uncomfortable defeat was suffered, the Welsh All Blacks winning 22–11 – a big score circa 1963. Four days later he was included in the team to play Gloucester, but when he ran out at Rodney Parade for what might have been his first home match for Newport, he had actually been there before and the memories came flooding back. It was an Easter Tuesday, possibly in 1956 or maybe 1957, and Newport were entertaining the Barbarians in the traditional holiday fixture. To keep the expected large crowd entertained, a curtain-raiser saw Newport Schools Under 16s play Maesteg Schools Under 16s and included at full-back in the Newport team was one Stuart Watkins. He remembers running out to a near empty stadium and ending the match in front of upwards of 15,000 spectators.

Those first two matches were the start of what would become a run of 19 consecutive appearances on the right wing for the recent arrival at the club, but it was not as straightforward as that might suggest. Confidence played a big part in Stuart Watkins' game and, despite the faith shown in him by the selectors, he was not seen to be doing himself justice. He remembers Brian Price taking him to one side and giving him a much needed talking to. Did he want to play against the All Blacks? If so, he was going to have to take stock, let his obvious talent show itself, make that right wing position his own. Stuart Watkins still relates how this quiet word from the club captain set him on his way to becoming an outstanding wing, not only for Newport but also for Wales and the British Lions. Brian Price may not remember it, but Stuart Watkins has never forgotten it – one of the minor issues that make a fine captain perhaps?

With the departure of John Anderson, the need of a second-choice blind-side wing forward to act as cover for Brian Cresswell was another problem that needed addressing. At some stage new blood was going to have to be introduced and, for the visit of Gloucester, the selectors decided to take the plunge giving supporters a second new player to rule the thumb over. David Nash was the first forward from Ebbw Vale to be capped by Wales when he made his debut against South Africa in 1960. Two years later, he toured that country with the British Lions, so when such an experienced player identifies a young prospect it makes sense to listen. An invitation to take part in Ebbw Vale's trial match was received by a young man playing on the open-side of the back row for his local club, Blaenavon. As luck would have it, work commitments prevented him travelling over the valley to Eugene Cross Park, and a few days later Keith Poole decided to try his luck at Newport.

Unaware of any unwritten pecking order, Poole arrived at Rodney Parade, headed up the stairs to what was the home dressing room, claimed a peg and went to the loo. On his return, his clothes were on the floor and an irate Brian Cresswell told the young whippersnapper in no uncertain terms to take himself off downstairs to the visitors dressing room and only return to the inner sanctum when he had earned the right to do so. Undeterred, Poole went about his business on the pitch and did enough to be selected to play for Newport United a week later. Barely four weeks into the season Keith Poole got the call he was hoping for when he was included in the team to play Gloucester. David Jones, Graham Bevan and Neville Johnson were in the front row, Brian Price and Ian Ford packing down behind, and alongside Glyn Davidge and Algy Thomas in the back row was Keith Poole. This was the first time the eight forwards played together as a unit, with Poole's inclusion allowing an opportunity to rest Brian Cresswell. Newport defeated Gloucester 6–3 and in doing so avoided a third consecutive defeat on the back of visits to Bristol, and Neath. Three days later, Cresswell returned to the team that drew with Swansea, while Poole returned to the United but, the youngster had eaten at the top table, enjoyed it and undoubtedly wanted more. The first of his record-breaking 486 appearances in a Newport jersey was under his belt. Who knew when the second would come along, but when it did Keith Poole would be ready.

The arrival of New Zealand at Rodney Parade may have been over a month away but when the tickets went on general sale, so too did interest in the match begin to escalate. Members of the club were automatically granted admission to all home games, but the season ticket did not cover matches against touring sides. The WRU had laid down the pricing criteria when the fixtures were first announced and it was going to cost 10/– (50p) to sit in the grandstand, 4/– to stand in the enclosure, 3/– in the field and 2/– would get schoolboys into a designated area. Demand for tickets in the first few weeks suggested the match would be a sell out, which would see a crowd of almost 25,000 fill Rodney Parade on the day. Such was the interest in the All Blacks, the BBC negotiated a deal to cover the second half of the match live on television with similar arrangements in place for the meeting with Cardiff in November. Coverage would only be received in Wales and for this the broadcaster paid £1,000 for the Cardiff match which was to take place on a Saturday, while Newport's midweek fixture was expected to reach fewer homes and therefore only deemed to be worth £350.

On 10 October the WRU ratified several transfer requests, among them that of Keith Poole from Blaenavon to Newport, Stuart Watkins from Cross Keys to Newport and Byron Thomas from Newport to Cardiff. Two days later Newport travelled to London to play Blackheath in the ninth match of the season, by which time 29 players had made first-team appearances. The following week the number would be 30, but the new name did not come from the squad of Newport United players, but much further from home.

Peter Wright was a loose-head prop who played his club rugby at Blackheath, had won 13 consecutive England caps and toured South Africa with the British Lions in 1962. Also on the tour to South Africa was Bryn Meredith and the Newport hooker was well acquainted with Peter Wright and would have packed down alongside him on more than one occasion. Wright didn't play against Newport, but the following week, he did play for the Black and Ambers, twice in fact. Peter Wright played in the home victory against Pontypool and the defeat at Gloucester, all of which is a matter of record. What isn't clear is if he was introduced into the team with the New Zealand match in mind, now less than two weeks away. David Jones was given no explanation when he was dropped in favour of Wright, whose inclusion meant moving Neville Johnson over to the tight-head in an experiment that was doomed from the start.

Newport fielded the same team against Pontypool and Gloucester, not only the first time this had happened during the current season but the first time it had happened during the year. Such apparent inconsistent consistency was viewed by many as a clear pointer to the team that would start against New Zealand. Cheney had returned at full-back, Perrott got the nod over Peter Rees on the left wing, Dick Uzzell was able to get away from St Luke's to play alongside Brian Jones in both matches and David Watkins was back from injury to partner Prosser. Graham Bevan took his place in the middle of the rearranged front row, with Price and Ford in the boiler house – Thomas, Davidge and Cresswell packing down behind them. Which was fine until Neville Johnson decided he was not comfortable on the tight-head of the scrum and would prefer life back on the loose-head. All of which led to Peter Wright's departure from Rodney Parade, which was as speedy as had been his unexpected arrival all of seven days earlier. Now all that stood between Newport and the arrival of the All Blacks was a home match against the Wasps which saw David Jones return to the front row and Eddie Mogford included in the centre in place of Dick Uzzell who had picked up an injury playing against Gloucester. Somewhere, among all the debris, there was a team of some significance beginning to emerge, all the selectors had to do was identify the 15 players involved in its make-up.

In 1963 the only coach that Newport RFC would have been in contact with was the one that took the team to away matches. Training sessions fell pretty much under the auspices of the captain, helped by senior players and watched from the touchlines by representatives of the selection committee. When the club involved Bryn Meredith, Ian McJennett and Bryn Williams to help prepare the team for the biggest match of the season, the trio took their responsibilities very seriously indeed. Were they coaches? Not in the modern understanding of the word, rather consultants acting in an advisory capacity. Whatever handle is attached to them the end result was the same, the former players adding their expertise and know-how to the mix with Meredith and McJennett helping the forwards, Williams focussing on the back play – and didn't they do well?

Bryn Meredith has already been discussed, but it is worth reiterating that he was the finest hooker of his generation and arguably one of the best of all time. He had toured New Zealand and had first-hand experience regarding how an All Blacks' pack went about its business. Ian McJennett was a familiar face in the Newport front row during the 1950s, at a time when Bryn Williams was an outstanding centre for the club. The only problem facing this unofficial coaching team was their lack of knowledge about the players they were preparing a team to face. This could be rectified by watching New Zealand in the flesh and there were only going to be two opportunities to do that. The first match of the tour was against Oxford University, after which the All Blacks would play the Southern Counties at Hove. And so it came about that on the morning of Wednesday, 23 October, a group of delegates from Newport set off for Oxford to get that all-important first look at the tourists.

CHAPTER FOUR

Getting Ready

"Fail to prepare, prepare to fail."
Source unknown

COME THE END of October ten members of the gang involved in the Great Train Robbery were behind bars awaiting trial and two more would be arrested before the end of the year. Charlie Wilson, William Boal and Roger Cordrey were caught within a matter of weeks; Ronnie Biggs and Gordon Goodey would soon join them. Not one of the main players in the robbery, Biggs' notoriety would reach new heights when, having been handed a 30-year sentence, he escaped from Wandsworth Prison in July 1965 and remained at large for the next 36 years. Buster Edwards and Bruce Reynolds had longer than most to enjoy the fruits of their labours but life on the run got the better of Edwards who gave himself up in September 1966, and two years later Reynolds was the last of the robbers to be brought to justice – five others remain at large.

The dust may have settled following the Profumo Affair but Harold Macmillan's assertion that no British government should be brought down by two tarts looked more than a tad optimistic when the prime minister resigned from office on 18 October. Ill health prompted his decision but, for the Conservative party, Macmillan's resignation signalled the beginning of the end. He was replaced by Alec Douglas-Home, who relinquished his seat in the House of Lords to take up office, the fourth Conservative prime minister in an extended period which began with Winston Churchill in 1951, then Anthony Eden who in turn was followed by Macmillan. Douglas-Home's time at Number Ten would last a year, the Labour party under Harold Wilson winning the general election of October 1964 by a narrow overall majority, four seats determining the outcome.

Harold Wilson was a Yorkshireman by birth, Huddersfield his home town before the family relocated to the Wirral, not a stone's throw from Liverpool, the home of the seismic cultural movement that started in the early months of 1963. The impact popular music could have on a generation was probably first seen during the 1950s with the advent of rock 'n' roll. Later years would highlight other examples of music exerting an overriding influence on the youth of the day, but none of them can be compared to that which first reared its head in 1963 and during the remaining years of the decade managed to change society forever.

The 'old guard' showed some resistance. The Shadows' 'Dance On' was knocked off the top of the charts by the ex-Shadows duo Jet Harris and Tony Meehan, who continued the instrumental trend with 'Diamonds'. These offerings denied the Beatles' 'Please Please Me' the number one spot and when the Aussie crooner Frank Ifield stormed to the top of the charts with 'The Wayward Wind' to be replaced three weeks later by Cliff Richard's 'Summer Holiday' the four Liverpudlians were going to have to wait for that first chart-topping single. This would cause much debate and argument in years to come, as independent charts published by various music papers did show the Beatles at number one with 'Please Please Me' but the overriding Top 40 compiled by the trade paper *Record Retailer* begged to differ and it is that publication's listings that have become the accepted point of reference.

The chart published for the week ending 11 April confirmed that a Liverpool group had made it to the number one spot, but not the Fab Four. When it arrived, the Merseybeat domination of the music charts was led by Gerry and the Pacemakers with a catchy number called 'How Do You Do It?' which held pole position for three weeks. On 2 May and at the third attempt, John, Paul, George and Ringo claimed the first of many number one hit singles when 'From Me To You' knocked Gerry and the Pacemakers off the top and continued as the UK's best selling disc for the next seven weeks. Liverpool's growing dominance of the pop music scene continued when Gerry Marsden and his Pacemakers toppled the Beatles with 'I Like It', spending four weeks at number one before Frank Ifield confirmed that he was not going to go down without a fight. 'I'm Confessin' (That I Love You)' and Elvis Presley's '(You're the) Devil in Disguise' can be bracketed together (literally) as the two discs that interrupted eight months of chart supremacy by the new wave of groups that predominantly hailed from the north of England.

'Sweets For My Sweet' from the Searchers toppled the King and when 'Bad to Me' by Billy J. Kramer and the Dakotas replaced them at number one, it was no little compensation as their first offering 'Do You Wanna Know a Secret?' had peaked at number two, denied by 'From Me To You'. When the Beatles released 'She Loves You', the year's defining moment in popular music had arrived. From that day on young men would seek out Chelsea boots in their local shoe shops, which were all the better if they had a seam stitched up the centre, but more importantly they had started to upset the establishment by growing their hair!

In 1962 the Beatles auditioned for Decca records. They played for an assistant in the A&R (Artists and Repertoire) department who later had to choose between them and Brian Poole and the Tremeloes, an Essex-based group who eventually got the nod. Time would prove how big a mistake that decision was but, in October 1963, it was the Decca signing who topped the charts with 'Do You Love Me?' Brian Poole and the Tremeloes joined a label that included American stars the Everly Brothers and Little Richard among its recording artists.

Those two great names from across the pond headlined a tour of the UK which arrived at Cardiff's Capital Theatre on 6 October and, included near the bottom of the bill, was a five-piece group recently signed by Decca. The Rolling Stones had flirted with the bottom half of the Top 40 for some weeks with their debut single 'Come On' but were about to lead popular music in another direction and would eventually more than recompense their masters at Decca for the opportunity missed by the label twelve months earlier.

Whether the drive to Oxford was accompanied by choruses of 'She Loves You', the introduction to 'Do You love Me?' – "You broke my heart, Cos I couldn't dance..." or was the driver encouraged to 'Come On' we will never know. One suspects that none of these alternatives made the journey, but we do know that on Wednesday, 23 October, a car set off from Newport taking Bryn Meredith, Brian Price, Brian Jones and Dick Uzzell to Oxford's Iffley Road for a first look at New Zealand in the opening match of their British tour.

Whether the players were fully recovered from the knock-on effects of a long and exhausting flight was an irrelevance. From that first kick-off there were to be no excuses – the All Blacks would have to stand or fall by how they performed on the field of play. Keen that the tour got off to a good start, the line-up included nine players who had featured in the second Test against England in June, including captain Wilson Whineray, Colin Meads, and Dennis Young up front with Ralph Caulton, Malcolm Dick and Don Clarke among the backs. They may well have been rusty, rough around the edges and far from the finished article, but New Zealand served up an impressive display and come the final whistle, there was little doubt as to where the tourist's strengths were to be found. They may well have tired towards the end but the forwards looked a force to be reckoned with, and were certain to improve as the tour progressed. And there was the mighty boot of Don Clarke.

The All Blacks ran out 19–3 winners with Clarke kicking 13 of his side's points, sending a resounding message to all future opponents – infringements will be punished. Final statistics of a distinguished playing career would show that the full-back scored nigh on ten points every time he pulled on a New Zealand jersey, more than enough to win many a match in the 1950s and 1960s. There was much to talk about on the journey back to Newport.

Customers at one of the service stations along the A48 must have wondered what was going on when casting an eye at the group of men sat around one of the tables that was covered with condiments. Several salt and pepper dispensers, together with sauce and vinegar bottles had been commandeered from the surrounding tables and lined up to represent opposing teams, moved around the table and positioned as required – chess of a very different kind. How was the All Blacks' threat from the peel off at the back of a line-out to be countered? What was the best way of controlling the ball when it was on the ground? How to contain the foot rushes? And what to do about Don Clarke who was not only a threat with the boot but a formidable man to have to stop if he was allowed to get into full stride?

From the outset it had been the intention of the New Zealand management that all 30 players would have made at least one appearance after three matches. With this in mind the team selected to play the Southern Counties at Hove in the second match showed 13 changes. Only Don Clarke and second-row Allan Stewart retained their places and it was Ian Clarke who took over the captaincy. This left just two players yet to appear in the starting line-up; second row Stan Meads, who had needed minor surgery for the removal of a boil shortly after arriving in the UK, and outside-half Earle Kirton.

As expected, the combined side were no match for a New Zealand team that stepped up a gear from the opening match, scoring five tries in the 32 points to 3 victory. Rather uncharacteristically, Don Clarke missed four of the conversions but three penalty goals and two drop goals were confirmation enough that his presence on a field was a constant threat to all opponents who deemed fit to transgress the laws. The full-back registered 17 of New Zealand's points, bringing his total to 30 from the first two games.

Watching on with particular interest were Ian McJennett and former Newport, Wales and British Lions hooker 'Bunner' Travers, who had recently stood down as club chairman. The pair had travelled to the south coast with the brief to cast an eye over those players who had not featured in the opening match. Newport RFC was certainly doing its homework, hoping to identify any weaknesses but, after two comfortable victories, other than confirming what was already common knowledge, the All Blacks had given nothing away. With the tour off to a good start, the road now led west and to Wales, the party arriving at the Seabank Hotel in Porthcawl on Sunday, which would serve as their base for the next three matches.

As the All Blacks were getting into their stride at Hove, Newport played the Wasps at Rodney Parade. The restored equilibrium in the front row was the only adjustment to the side that played against Pontypool and Gloucester, with the exception of a new partner for Brian Jones in the centre. Eddie Mogford came in for Dick Uzzell who was struggling with a pulled hamstring that was beginning to give cause for concern. The Newport team to play New Zealand had not been confirmed in the press, but on Saturday morning 15 players assembled at Rodney Parade for the team photograph that would be included in the match day programme. There were no surprise selections: David Jones, Graham Bevan, Neville Johnson, Ian Ford, Brian Price, Algy Thomas, Glyn Davidge and Brian Cresswell were named up front with Bob Prosser, David Watkins, John Uzzell, Brian Jones, Dennis Perrott, Stuart Watkins and Ray Cheney expected to pose some problems for the tourists behind the scrum.

Following Peter Wright's departure, the only position that might have presented the selectors with any extended deliberations was that of left wing. Should they opt for the barnstorming approach of the outstanding Peter Rees, or include the quicker Perrott, who could introduce that sudden injection of pace found in the make-up of a top-class sprinter. The choice cannot have been easy. Peter Rees joined Newport from Newbridge at the start of the 1960–1 season. He made an immediate impression that did not escape the attention of the Welsh selectors, and won three caps in that season's championship. Although he was a confirmed left wing, the position belonged to Swansea's Dewi Bebb leaving the selectors no choice other than to play Rees on the right. Ironically, it was an injury sustained by Bebb that led to him getting an opportunity to play for Wales in his preferred position when winning a fourth cap three years later.

If Peter Rees' credentials ever needed rubber-stamping, then one need look no further than his performances in the black and amber jersey. During eleven seasons with Newport, he made 330 appearances which included all 51 matches of the 1967–8 campaign, a remarkable feat of consistency and endurance. And Rees was not shy when it came to doing what wings do best, scoring 157 tries for the club. Little wonder then that Peter Rees was a firm favourite among the thousands of spectators that followed Newport during the 1960s, but there was a decision to be made and it must have been a great disappointment when the Newport selection committee handed the number eleven jersey to Dennis Perrott.

The list of players who can relate stories of what might have been is endless. Injuries have forced many to miss out on selection, or even worse – be selected, then have to withdraw at the eleventh hour. Then the proverbial insult would be added in spades when said player is subjected to watching his side record a famous victory from a seat in the grandstand. That he was in good company would have been no consolation to Brian Cresswell, who was injured playing against the Wasps on Saturday and forced to withdraw from the team selected for Wednesday's match.

It was all quite innocuous really. From a restart the ball was claimed by the Newport forwards but a clumsy effort by the Wasps number eight was all that was needed to upset the best-laid plans. Cresswell twisted awkwardly, the forward fell across him and the Newport player took the full weight of the impact on his left knee. With the player lying prone on the ground, Newport physio Gerry Lewis was quickly out of the blocks and at his side. Magic sponge in hand, he set about assessing the damage and easing the pain. With 15 minutes remaining, Cresswell decided he was able to carry on, Lewis concurred and Newport saw out the match with a full complement of players. It goes without saying that this was a huge mistake, but it is also certain that the injury sustained would have prevented the player taking his place against the All Blacks even if he had left the field. The medial ligaments were seriously damaged and, much as Gerry Lewis tried to improve the situation, he was fighting a lost cause. Medial ligaments don't repair themselves in 48 hours which was all the time Brian Cresswell had at his disposal to convince the selectors, and more importantly himself, that he would be able to play on Wednesday. At Monday's training session, Cresswell confirmed to Bill Everson that he would not be able to take his place against New Zealand, a decision that had to be made but which remains the toughest in the Newport back-row forward's long and illustrious career.

Cresswell had joined Newport in 1956 and quickly established himself as first choice on the blind side of the scrum. Alongside Glyn Davidge and Geoff Whitson, he formed an outstanding breakaway unit, each player knowing exactly what was expected of him in every conceivable situation. This appears to be all too obvious, but few of the club's back-row combinations had operated with such expertise or were better organised as they went about their business than that of Whitson, Davidge and Cresswell. Recognising this, the Welsh selectors chose them en bloc against Scotland and Ireland in 1960. Both matches were won, but Whitson was absent from the Welsh team against the French in the final match of the championship that saw Cresswell win the last of his four caps.

The coming weeks would reveal the long-term effects of Cresswell's untimely injury, which brought an immediate and totally unexpected end to his long run as a Newport player. One minute you are joining 14 other players in the official photograph of the team to play New Zealand, and the next you are limping back to the changing rooms knowing full well that only a miracle would see that same 15 take the field. Some reports suggested Brian Cresswell had been dropped by Newport, which is nonsense and easily dismissed by virtue of the fact that the photograph of the team as originally selected appeared in the match programme. Either way, this was a tragic set of circumstances for the player who was looking forward to completing a hat-trick, having played for the club against Australia in 1957 and South Africa in 1961. Here was one spectator who was going to watch the match with very mixed emotions.

Cresswells' untimely injury aside, the final dress rehearsal against the Wasps may have produced an eleven points to nil victory, but it was an uninspiring performance. How Newport could conjure up the wherewithal to down the tourists was a conundrum even the most partisan supporters would fail to unravel as they descended on the clubhouse for the customary post-mortem. It was all doom and gloom as the night rolled on, only the beer priced at approximately 1/3 a pint helping to raise moral. One shilling and three pence a pint? Even making allowances for inflation and modern-day values, six and a half pence in today's terms equates to 15 pints of ale for a pound with change – maybe Harold Macmillan was right.

Two weeks earlier in a conversation with Brian Price, the *Daily Telegraph*'s rugby correspondent John Reason revealed his thoughts when confirming that he had all but written off the club's chances of beating the tourists, telling the captain that Newport would do better if they were to challenge them to a round of golf. Sometimes it's better to be the underdog, not to be burdened by any great expectancy, but with such negative undercurrents beginning to surface outside the camp, it was time to put the barricades up, circle the wagons and do some serious soul searching.

With Cresswell's replacement yet to be confirmed, there now appeared to be doubts concerning the fitness of Dick Uzzell – would another late change have to be made? This was going to go to the wire, a real eleventh hour moment. Uzzell had pulled a hamstring at Gloucester and, after returning to St Luke's, he decided that his time would be better spent back in Newport where he could get the necessary treatment that would allow him to take the field against New Zealand. Various stories would feature in the press in the coming weeks regarding Uzzells' absence from college, the excuses offered and the punishment meted out, but most of them are inaccurate in all but the most salient points; that Dick Uzzell played against New Zealand and that he scored the drop goal that won the match.

For many years Newport RFC had benefited from the services of Ray Lewis, a well-regarded physiotherapist who performed wonders on stricken players who made their way to his practice for repair work. Now retired, Ray Lewis had been succeeded by his son Gerry, whose name would later become synonymous with Welsh rugby and all things pulled, strained, twisted or broken. Word that he was the top man in his field was yet to reach beyond Newport, but Dick Uzzell had no doubts concerning where he should head for treatment and, immediately on arriving at Newport railway station, he headed off in search of the magic hands that would hopefully put him right.

The initial prognosis was not good and, with little more than a week in which to repair the damage, Lewis wanted to see his new patient twice a day if he was to have any chance of getting him fit enough to take part in what promised to be a particularly physical game. Remember, there were no replacements allowed at the time. If Uzzell was forced to leave the field, Newport would have to continue with 14 men, a risk that could not be taken. To make life a little easier, rather than returning to the family home in Bargoed, Uzzell took up temporary residence at his cousin's new home in Caldicot, a short distance from Newport and the physio's couch where he was destined to spend much of his time in the coming days. After a morning session with Lewis, Dick Uzzell would more often than not spend the hours before his afternoon appointment at Rodney Parade. He would go to the club, find a quiet corner in one of the dressing rooms and catnap before returning for the afternoon massage and manipulation.

The Newport team, as originally selected, together with the coaches and club officials met at Rodney Parade on the Sunday following the Wasps match. This was unheard of in the days of amateur rugby, but it was essential those players who had not seen the All Blacks play received a thorough debrief from those who had. This was the time to discuss the tactics which were to be employed and could be practised time and time again at the two training sessions arranged for Monday and Tuesday.

Fifty years on it is difficult to relate to a period when television coverage of rugby rarely reached beyond international matches. That the BBC would be showing the second half of Newport and Cardiff's games against the All Blacks was a huge step forward. Clearly there was no video footage to analyse, so preparing for a match against players that most of the Newport team were not familiar with cannot have been easy. And while the tourists were yet to confirm the team that would play Newport, it was still very much a case of fail to prepare, prepare to fail. Word of mouth was one thing, but seeing an opponent in the flesh was a very different proposition. One could argue that 14 or 15 stones in a six-foot frame was much like any other 14 or 15 stones in a six-foot frame. There were many such specimens to be found throughout Wales, but it was how the individual went about his business on the field that would set some apart.

Then there was the added problem that concerned the mindset of these men from down under – what went on between the ears? Impossible to assess from the touchline, this aspect of New Zealand rugby was as much a mystery to onlookers in 1963 as it remains today, and one suspects that the only way to get anywhere near understanding what makes New Zealand rugby the global force it has always been is to encounter its finest players on a rugby pitch, get in among them, feel the contact, seek out any weaknesses and turn them to advantage. Those weaknesses did exist, there were chinks in the armour, but the big problem facing Newport was that there would only be the one chance to find them, exploit them and punish them. There would be no second bite of the cherry.

Brian Price is more than happy to describe Newport's basic strategy as being somewhat negative. Various aspects of New Zealand's play had been identified, and plans needed to be put in place to counter those areas on which the All Blacks would be relying. It was certain that Wilson Whineray, who was expected to play after being rested against the Southern Counties, would regularly peel off the tail of the line-out in company with the tight-head prop, and it would be for David Jones and Neville Johnson to make sure that they went with them, bringing the ball carrier to ground before the movement gained any momentum. The last thing Newport wanted was for half-backs Bob Prosser and David Watkins to be involved in any unnecessary tackling, and it would be the responsibility of the back row and centres to cover for them as much as possible. Clearly the pair could not be wrapped in cotton wool but, they were critical to Newport's kicking game which would see Don Clarke, also likely to be included, turned at every opportunity, sent running back to the corners to retrieve the strategically placed kicks put up by Prosser from the base of the scrum or Watkins in his position a little further away from the forwards.

Any ball collected from a kick ahead was to be marked. Today, this chance to calm things down is restricted to balls fielded inside the 22-metre area of the field, but such dispensation once extended to all parts of the field and, whether it be from one of the box kicks favoured by the All Blacks or a mighty hoof from the full-back, the instruction was to take a clean catch, call a mark, then return the kick with interest. And while on the subject of kicks – discipline was to be the order of the day. Discipline, discipline, discipline – no penalties to be given away within 60 yards of the Newport goal line. None. Not even a number that could be counted on the fingers of one hand, that was far too many!

New Zealand was also known to favour foot rushes by the forwards as a way of advancing play and, if the weather proved to be unkind and rain fell during the match, this tactic would certainly be introduced. The only defence was to kill the ball at source, fall on it, risk life and limb at the feet of eight big men who could be guaranteed to take no prisoners. This unenviable task would largely be the responsibility of Glyn Davidge who revelled in getting to grips with the ball on the floor. It would be left to the referee to decide if any player was in breach of the laws, and there were sure to be some disputed calls, but Davidge was the man for such occasions. Much would depend on his disruptive powers when the ball was inches from the grass. A big responsibility in such a physical contest, and one which would need to be carried out to perfection because if Davidge was deemed to step over the mark, thereby presenting Clarke with kicks at goal, it would be game over. Much was expected from the Newport team, and perhaps even more from an inexperienced young man from Blaenavon who to this day insists that in October 1963 he hadn't the faintest idea who the All Blacks were.

Keith Poole was at Blaenavon Rugby Club on Sunday when he received a telephone call from Cyril Williams, a Newport committee member, asking him to attend a training session to be held at the club on Monday evening. At a meeting, held earlier in the day, it was looking extremely unlikely that Brian Cresswell would be able to take his place in the team come Wednesday. If that were to be confirmed, what options were available? Two alternatives were considered. A recent recruit at Newport was second-row forward Bill Morris, who could also play at number eight if required, and including him in that position was the first option tabled. The downside of this would see Glyn Davidge playing on the blind side of the scrum, a position in marked contrast to that of number eight, and where he would be expected to play a very different game. If Davidge was spending his time harassing the backs, flirting with the off-side line and testing the referee's patience as all good wing forwards were expected to do, he would be unable to get into those areas where life and limb were at risk and it was unlikely that Morris could be used in the same way. Plan B saw a straight replacement for Cresswell being introduced, the reason Keith Poole was asked to train with the team on Monday.

Following that training session, it was confirmed that a player who had made only one first-team appearance was about to make his second. When one loses sight of the facts and allow stories bordering on myth and legend to cloud the memory bank, then over the process of time such facts become distorted but remain taken as read. Such a case was that of the much reported 19 year old who played for Newport against New Zealand in 1963. Keith Poole was born on 2 October 1943 and, much as a story of a teenager playing in such a big match might have made for better headlines, the fact of the matter is that Poole was now 20 years old.

Whatever his age, the inclusion of Keith Poole was certainly newsworthy, and the local press was intent on featuring him in the pages of the edition that would hit the stands on the eve of the match. Where did he work? Good question, but while the answer was GKN, a steel processing plant in Cwmbrân, what he did there was another matter. Three weeks earlier Keith Poole joined the company after being introduced by

Cyril Williams. The main attraction about the offer was, rather than the eight-hour shifts he was familiar with, Poole would now work a straight Monday to Friday, allowing him to train regularly and play in any midweek matches when selected. Nobody had yet decided where he should spend his working day and the first three weeks saw him carrying out a variety of odd-jobs, but for the purposes of a photograph Keith Poole became a blacksmith, seen in the forge with hammer in hand, wearing all the necessary aprons and regalia associated with the task of shaping metal.

New Zealand had used 28 of the 30-man squad in the first two matches. With Stan Meads still unavailable, only outside-half Earle Kirton had yet to play and his inclusion against Newport seemed certain. The big question was how strong a team would the All Blacks field? How many of the big names would play at Rodney Parade? Depending on one's viewpoint, the New Zealand selectors certainly did the Welsh club proud when it announced the line-up.

Wilson Whineray would lead the side from the front row, packing down on the loose head. The captain may have been criticised for his ability in the scrum, but as Colin Meads later commented, "it is hard to recall a time when our scrum, suffered because of any weakness... as a captain he inspired fierce loyalty". Some years later, respected New Zealand rugby correspondent Terry McLean wrote, "I would unhesitatingly acclaim him as New Zealand's greatest captain".

Joining Whineray in the front row were Ian Clarke on the tight-head and hooker John Major. Clarke was New Zealand's most capped player at the time, an honour he shared with brother Don. He had previous experience of Rodney Parade, having played against Newport in 1954, and was the only one of the current party who had toured with the fourth All Blacks. When the teams took to the field on Wednesday, he would recognise centre Brian Jones who had played for Newport on the day. That match had taken place on a Thursday in front of an estimated 20,000 spectators, a figure that would be significantly more this time around. Barring injury, John Major would have to accept his lot as number two in the pecking order behind Dennis Young but, with seasoned internationals either side of him, the Newport front row were going to have their work cut out in the scrum.

Ron Horsley was a second-row forward who knew what it was like to spend months on the road, having toured South Africa with the All Blacks in 1960 playing in three Test matches. Horsley's participation in the current tour would be put on hold when he had to have his appendix removed after playing in twelve of the first 20 matches but he enjoyed one final run out in the jersey when the tourists played British Columbia in Vancouver on the journey home. However, it was Horsley's partner in the boiler house who would attract the most attention, both from the opposing forwards and the thousands of spectators packed into the ground.

Colin Meads was a player whose reputation preceded him. He made his international debut in 1957 and would win the last of 55 caps in 1972. Pinetree was described as "a terrible man with the silver fern on... he stood alone as the greatest player I have ever known" by Fergie McCormick, a New Zealand full-back of the late 1960s. An opponents' perspective is offered by Willie John McBride who says "Yes, he was a tough bastard but the bugger had a good side to him... Meads always wanted to win but he was prepared to acknowledge the better team when the mighty All Blacks fell". And closer to home, from Gareth Edwards, "the big fellow's roughness on the field adds up to so little when you think of the tremendous amount of physical energy he poured into every match he played". Fellow tourist in 1963, scrum-half Chris Laidlaw, profiled Meads on his being confirmed as New Zealand's Player of the Century – "He's a great man... it would have been ridiculous if the award went to anyone else", before going on to confirm that "Meads delivered many a punch that was seen by the referee and a good deal more that were not". The depths of the scrum and maul were dark places to visit circa 1963, and it is highly unlikely that Colin Earl Meads was alone in his use of fisticuffs on occasion. Whatever shenanigans may or may not occur, the Newport forwards were going to have to be seen to be on their best behaviour, whiter than white – no penalties the abiding message of the day.

Meads and Horsley both stood at 6' 4" and behind them were two others who topped the six-foot mark. At 6' 3" number eight Brian Lochore was yet to make his mark as one of his country's great players and captains but would win his first cap later in the tour. On the open side of the scrum was Kel Tremain, all of 6' 2" in his stockinged feet and another with Test-match experience that had started against the British Lions in 1959. Making up the eight was a relative newcomer, Auckland open-side wing forward Waka Nathan. Since winning his first cap in 1962, Nathan had been ever present in the back row and was described by Colin Meads as "the most virile runner with the ball in hand". Like Horsley, Nathan would miss a large part of the tour after breaking his jaw when playing against Llanelli, but on 30 October at Rodney Parade he took his place alongside Tremain and Lochore in a back row still recognised as among the finest ever to play for New Zealand.

Not considered particularly big by today's standards but, by averaging over 15 stone per man and with five players standing over six feet tall, the New Zealand pack that was selected to play Newport was regarded as huge at the time. They were expected to dominate the opposition in the tight and their explosive presence in the loose would surely cause havoc among the backs. It used to be said that in open play you could cover eight New Zealand forwards with a blanket, so well did they function as a unit, and this particular selection looked capable of living up to that reputation. A total irrelevance at the time, but years later Wilson Whineray, Colin Meads and Brian Lochore would each receive knighthoods, which says much about the contribution these fine players made to the game.

Behind the scrum the selectors opted for a mix of experience and raw, young talent. Tour vice-captain and scrum-half Kevin Briscoe was chosen to partner Earle Kirton for the outside-half's first appearance in an All Black jersey. Centre Pat Walsh's international career dated back to 1955, making him the perfect partner for Ian MacRae who made his first appearance for New Zealand at Hove, a try adding to the celebrations. Another to get his name on the score sheet against the Southern Counties and also making his New Zealand debut on the day, was right wing Bill Davis. Despite the experienced Ralph Caulton being included on the left wing, the back line could be viewed as suspect until one considered the man completing the line-up at full-back. Don Clarke would play at Rodney Parade. Any hopes that the goal-kicking machine would be given a day off after playing in the first two matches were dashed when top of the team sheet was the man who would have number one on his back.

When the teams took the field the Newport players would be wearing jerseys with the recently revised sequence of numbering which now started with the loose-head prop wearing number one through to the full-back who had number 15 on his back. Gone were the days when the reverse was favoured with the sole exception of the omission of number 13 which meant a loose forward would have 16 on his back – a nod towards the number 13 being regarded by some as an unlucky omen. On which point, had anyone picked up on the fact that the match against New Zealand was the club's thirteenth of the season? – triskaidekaphobia abounding! In marked contrast, the All Blacks would wear their tour numbers. This meant Whineray could be identified by the number 17 on the back of his jersey, Meads picked out by number 22, Ian Clarke wore 18, with brother Don easily spotted by that single digit stretched across his broad back. In this unusual identity parade, only Earle Kirton would be instantly recognisable to spectators as it was the first five-eighths lot to be allocated the number ten jersey, the one normally associated with outside-halves and without doubt the most famous jersey number in Welsh rugby.

For many years neutral touch judges have assisted the referee in controlling the game. Their impartiality is now seen as essential in the search for fair play. They were a much more trusting lot in 1963, with the WRU and its counterparts more than happy to allow a representative of each team to take on the decision making when it came to where the ball left the field of play and who was responsible for its departure. Similarly, these two individuals would determine the success, or otherwise, of a kick at goal. Running the line for New Zealand would be back-row forward John Graham, with fixture secretary Nick Carter Newport's representative with the flag.

On the eve of the match the public were advised that very few tickets were left. The grandstand had long since been sold out and, with the weather forecast suggesting it would rain, those who hoped to get their hands on one knew they would be standing on the banks behind the posts where there was no cover to be had. Wednesday would prove how the public enjoyed sport, how people were prepared to turn out in numbers if the occasion warranted.

For a town with a population around the 100,000 mark, Newport boasted two large sporting venues, both found east of the River Usk. Rodney Parade is a stone's throw from the river but, a little further out of town was Somerton Park, the home of Newport County FC who were currently to be found in Division Four of the Football League. Since 1932, Somerton Park had also been a venue for greyhound racing, with meetings regularly held on Tuesdays and Fridays, which avoided clashing with those held at Cardiff Arms Park on Mondays and Saturdays.

A.P. Herbert's poem 'Don't let's go to the dogs tonight' would have little meaning in Newport after Tuesday, 29 October, because the option to visit the town's greyhound track would no longer be there. For nigh on 31 years, a night at the dogs had proved to be a popular diversion among the local populace, but sadly not enough of them were showing an interest come 1963, and the night before the town's rugby team played one of the most important matches in its long history, the hare set on its way with six dogs in chase for the last time. Those Newport folk who enjoyed their sport needed a fillip – best get to Rodney Parade and see if there were any tickets left!

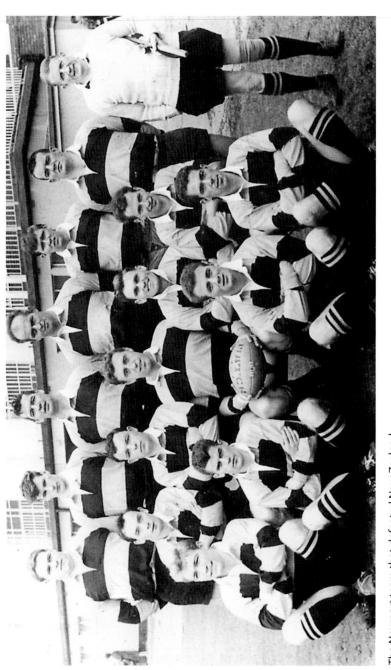

The Newport team that defeated New Zealand.
Back row: David Jones, Keith Poole, Glyn Davidge, Ian Ford, Stuart Watkins, Neville Johnson, Nick Carter (touch judge). Seated: Dennis Perrott, Graham Bevan, Brian Price (captain), Brian Jones, Ray Cheney. Front row: Alan Thomas, David Watkins, Bob Prosser, Dick Uzzell.
Photo: courtesy of Newport RFC

The Fifth All Blacks

Back row: C.R. Laidlaw, W.L. Davis, D.J. Graham, R.W. Caulton, P.F. Little, J.M. Le Lievre, W.J. Nathan, I.S.T. Smith, P.T. Walsh.

Middle row: I.R. MacRae, K.E. Barry, K.A. Nelson, S.T. Meads, C.E. Meads, A.J. Stewart, R.H. Horsley, B.J. Lochore, K.F. Gray, K.R. Tremain.

Seated: D.A. Arnold, I.J. Clarke, D.B. Clarke, K.C. Briscoe, F.D. Kilby (manager), W.J. Whineray (captain), N.J. McPhail (assistant manager), D. Young, E.W. Kirton, J. Major, M.J. Dick. Front row: B.A. Watt, M.A. Herewini

Photo: courtesy of New Zealand RFC

NEWPORT
RUGBY
FOOTBALL
CLUB

The cover of the match programme which remains a much sought-after piece of Newport RFC memorabilia and will cost a collector much more than the cover price of one shilling (5p in current monetary values).

New Zealand
v.
Newport

WEDNESDAY
OCTOBER 30th
1963

OFFICIAL
PROGRAMME
ONE SHILLING

Kick-off 3 p.m.

NEW ZEALAND					**NEWPORT**	
Colours : All Black					Colours : Black and Amber	
D. B. CLARKE	(1)	Full Back		Full Back	R. CHENEY	(15)
R. W. CAULTON	(2)	Left Wing		Right Wing	S. WATKINS	(14)
P. T. WALSH	(8)	Left Centre		Right Centre	J. UZZELL	(13)
I. R. MACRAE	(7)	Right Centre		Left Centre	B. J. JONES	(12)
W. L. DAVIS	(6)	Right Wing		Left Wing	D. PERROTT	(11)
E. W. KIRTON	(10)	Outside Half		Outside Half	D. WATKINS	(10)
K. C. BRISCOE	(11)	Inside Half		Inside Half	W. R. PROSSER	(9)
W. J. WHINERAY (Capt.)	(17)	Forwards		Forwards	N. JOHNSON	(1)
J. MAJOR	(16)				G. BEVAN	(2)
I. J. CLARKE	(18)				D. JONES	(3)
R. H. HORSLEY	(20)				B. V. PRICE (Capt.)	(4)
C. E. MEADS	(22)				I. FORD	(5)
W. J. NATHAN	(25)				A. THOMAS	(6)
B. J. LOCHORE	(28)				G. DAVIDGE	(8)
K. R. TREMAIN	(30)				K. W. POOLE	(7)

Touch Judge : Mr. D. J. GRAHAM   Referee : Mr. G. WALTERS - Gowerton   Touch Judge : Mr. R. T. CARTER

NEXT HOME GAME : v. **Ebbw Vale** SATURDAY, 2nd NOVEMBER, 1963, Kick-off 3.15 p.m.

How the teams lined up. When the New Zealand team was announced few gave Newport any hope of victory. The numbers may have been alien to spectators but so too was the newly-introduced sequence worn by Newport which has stood the test of time and is still in use today.

"… Receiving the ball from Prosser the outside-half had three options available to him – pass to the waiting Brian Jones, kick for the corner or run. Watkins decided to run…" The break by David Watkins that led to the drop goal which proved to be the difference between the teams at the final whistle. Watkins has looped outside Brian Jones and Uzzell has little room to move in so the pass had to go to Stuart Watkins and the rest, as they say, is history.

Photo: courtesy of *Western Mail*

Neville Johnson raises his arms as Ian Ford and David Jones follow the ball's progress over the crossbar. As do All Blacks Kel Tremain, Ron Horsley, Brian Lochore, Waka Nathan, John Major, Ian Clarke and Wilson Whineray. Graham Bevan, Brian Price and Keith Poole can also be identified together with referee Gwynne Walters but Dick Uzzell is nowhere to be seen.

Photo: courtesy of *South Wales Evening Post*

Newport captain Brian Price demonstrates the art of jumping at the line-out. The jumper was not allowed any assistance in his quest for the ball and Price looks to have the better of his opposite number Ron Horsley on this occasion. Truth was, most opponents failed to contain Price in this facet of play at which the Newport captain had few equals.

Both Newport half-backs kicked superbly during the match. This time it is the turn of Bob Prosser to put the All Blacks under pressure as he chips the ball ahead from the base of the scrum. This effort was not intended to test Don Clarke, the full-back seen looking on from the other side of the scrum.

Off-side – what's that? Four All Blacks appear to be intent on taking play into their own 25 or has the Newport player on the ground together with Ian Ford overstepped the mark? This was one for Gwynne Walters to sort out.

New Zealand gained some ascendancy in the latter part of the match and on this occasion it is Earl Kirton who has made the break and seen looking for support out wide.

Keith Poole has New Zealand scrum-half Kevin Briscoe in his grasp. Glyn Davidge and Algy Thomas are well positioned to contest any loose ball if Briscoe's pass fails to find his outside-half. This reflects much of the afternoon's play with the Newport back row dominant against one of the finest trios ever to don the famous black jersey.

It was not an afternoon for enterprising three-quarter play but early in the match Newport left wing Dennis Perrott received the ball and decided to place a kick deep into New Zealand territory. Here he is watched by Bill Davis and Waka Nathan with Brian Lochore moving in to make the tackle.

The 25th anniversary of the victory was celebrated with a dinner held at Rodney Parade on Friday, 28 October 1988. For the 50th anniversary the calendar conveniently saw 30 October land on a Wednesday meaning the celebrations were held 50 years on to the day.

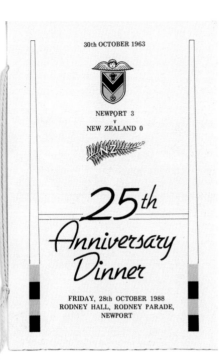

30th OCTOBER 1963

NEWPORT 3
v
NEW ZEALAND 0

25th
Anniversary
Dinner

FRIDAY, 28th OCTOBER 1988
RODNEY HALL, RODNEY PARADE,
NEWPORT

The team that never was. The match day programme included this photograph of the Newport team expected to take the field against New Zealand but for Brian Creswell (back row, second from the right) it was not to be, injury forcing him to stand down thereby giving Keith Poole his chance to join an elite group of players.

Photo: courtesy of Newport RFC

CHAPTER FIVE

Going to the Match

"Sometimes I have a sherry before dinner."
Charlie 'Bird' Parker (1920–55)

IT RAINED THROUGHOUT Tuesday and while Newport woke up to a dry Wednesday, grey clouds were gathered overhead and the prospect of more rain falling looked a racing certainty. This was it then. This was the day that had been earmarked in the sporting calendar of the town since those tour fixtures were announced way back in January. This was the day that all eyes would focus on a plot of land east of the river that had been the home of Newport RFC since 1877, when it was leased to what was then Newport Cricket, Athletic and Football Club by the Rt Hon. Lord Tredegar. That had been at a 'peppercorn rent' but in 1922 the opportunity for the Athletic Club to purchase the land had been taken and, for the princely sum of £7,026, an area comprising some 15 acres changed hands. Specifically, it was approximately one and a half of those acres which would become the focus of attention for a couple of hours on that Wednesday afternoon and anyone who hadn't got a ticket was not going to get anywhere near the place.

Newport welcomed the start of the day much like any other in that there was work to be done, school to attend, shopping to fetch and all manner of everyday chores to carry out but, for many, come lunchtime, normal routines were forgotten. The town centre was heaving as thousands of locals, together with people from further afield, arrived in search of sustenance before making the trek across the old town bridge to Rodney Parade. There were those who had taken a day from their holiday allocation, while others might have pulled strings and claimed an afternoon's leave. Shift workers may well have fallen lucky if they were working the 6 a.m. – 2 p.m. or 10 p.m. – 6 a.m. rotas, but for those working the hours between 2 p.m. – 10 p.m., it was a case of grin and bear it or make an unscheduled visit to the doctor, hope to pull the wool over his eyes and come away with the necessary certificate – chances were he was hoping to get to the match as well! For others, it was a case of throw caution to the wind, take the day off and just hope you didn't find yourself standing next to the boss on the terraces.

If you were still of school age that was fine. And if you were a school teacher that was fine as well. All schools in the borough of Newport closed at lunchtime, clearing the way for pupils and teachers alike to go to the match if so inclined. This was a grand gesture on the part of the local education committee, who had granted similar dispensation when previous touring sides had visited the town, a get-out-of-jail card that was usually kept for royal visits. Newport High School, west of the river, and St Julian's High School to the east, were two of Wales' leading seats of learning and at both institutions rugby football was the preferred winter sport for boys. Suffice to say that if these schools, in particular, had not been closed, there would have been a lot of empty desks for the afternoon lessons and a lot of white lies told the following morning.

Public houses in the centre of town and those within a brisk walk of Rodney Parade prepared themselves for what was certain to be a chaotic few hours before the match, and an equally busy evening session when they reopened their doors to customers either looking to celebrate in style or drown their sorrows with equal intensity. The days when a public house could extend its opening times to at least twelve hours a day were a long way off, but a few streetwise landlords had the foresight to apply to the local magistrates for an extension. Rather than having to wait until 5.30 p.m., the crowds leaving the ground at the final whistle would find the Ivy Bush in Clarence Place, the Carpenters Arms in the High Street and the Cross Keys in nearby Market Street among those hostelries that would fling open their doors an hour earlier. There was always the clubhouse, but this was largely the domain of members, and a squeeze into its bars was best avoided. There would be many a tale to tell about the after-match revelries and, as we have seen, a pound certainly bought a lot of beer. There weren't many who could accommodate such large quantities if so inclined to spend the week's budget in one hit but, judging by later reports of pubs running dry, it seems many a hardy soul went down trying! A bit more caution was needed before the match. Nobody wanted to get caught short among the massed congregation in the enclosure and the even greater numbers that would fill the terraces. This was going to be all about pacing and, at some point food would have to be taken on board, all of which would help when setting out on what promised to be a long night, whatever the outcome.

Food glorious food. Where did the demanding hordes that descended on the town head for the sustenance which would see them through the day? Truth be known, Newport has never been a gourmet's delight but in 1963 it was probably as good as at any other time. This was the era of the prawn cocktail, steak and chips and Black Forest gateau, all washed down with a bottle of Mateus Rose. Not that this particular vino was better than any other but it arrived in an attractive bottle which just cried out for a candle to be stuck in the top and, when lit, the wax allowed to decoratively work its way down the body of the bottle – a piece of creative art that adorned many a suitable resting place in the homes of the day. And where was such sophisticated fare to be found? The Berni Steak House was the place to go and Newport boasted two of these popular eating places; one found within the Tredegar Arms Hotel on the High

Street and the other at the Royal Albert Grill on Commercial Street.

Traditional fish and chips was the fare at the institution that was, and is, Vacaras in Llanarth Street, and for the more adventurous the New Moon Chinese restaurant would have a generous set lunch available for a few shillings. A glass of fruit juice was followed by a main course which invariably came served with a fried egg on top. Dessert might be either a banana or pineapple ring in batter and, if that didn't appeal, then a scoop of ice cream was an alternative, but this tended to be served in a metal dish which, for some reason, always seemed to be hot meaning the ice cream had melted by the time it arrived at the table. That aside, it was great value and ever popular with the lunchtime crowd. Like the New Moon, the Lahore Indian restaurant is another that was and remains a Newport institution, but its offerings were perhaps best put on hold until later in the day when the curry could be given the attention it fully deserved.

Somewhere among this cornucopia of gastronomic delights could be found the Wimpy Bar and Grill, the precursor of McDonald's and Burger King in the town. For a couple of bob you could go the whole hog and have the signature dish (a Wimpy was simply a beefburger in a bun), together with the interestingly named Bender, a bun with a frankfurter sausage grilled to curl round on itself and form a near circle, in the middle of which was a dollop of Branston Pickle with a slice of tomato on top – or did the tomato go in first? No matter. A serving of chips completed the platter and it was magic. Maybe a Coke Float to wash it all down and it was time to bring on those mighty All Blacks.

The tourists left Porthcawl mid-morning for the drive to Newport which, 50 years ago, may well have taken upwards of two hours. On arrival in the town, the team selected to play was deposited at the Westgate Hotel for a light lunch, while the rest of the party were royally entertained by the mayor of Newport, Councillor Trevor Vaughan, at a reception held in the Civic Centre. Also in attendance were some of the great names of Newport rugby, among them Ken Jones, Bob Evans and Malcolm Thomas who had toured New Zealand with the British Lions in 1950 and Jack Wetter, Newport's captain in the 1922–3 season when the club was invincible. Guest of honour was Sir Thomas L. MacDonald, the High Commissioner for New Zealand. For the Newport players there was no out-of-town meeting point from which they would be taken on to the ground thereby arriving as one, nor were there any specific instructions to observe. It was business as usual – be in the changing room an hour before the kick-off. Or else!

Twelve months earlier local schools had closed their doors on 26 October when the Queen, accompanied by Prince Philip, arrived in Newport to officially open the Richard, Thomas and Baldwin (RTB) steelworks, a massive development extending to over 2,500 acres and located at Llanwern, a few miles east of the town. During its construction, an estimated five million tons of shale was transported to the site, many of the lorries having to journey through the middle of Newport to cross the River Usk via the town bridge and often bringing traffic to a standstill. On 30 October, it was a sea of *bodies* that made life difficult for drivers trying to negotiate the bridge and, among its number, could be spotted Newport players who had to walk to Rodney Parade from the bus or train station. Ray Cheney was working at RTB at the time, a job that was governed by shifts and, on Wednesday, he was down to work the 2 p.m. – 10 p.m. slot which clearly presented the full-back with a problem. The simple solution was to swap but nobody would accommodate him. Why? They were all going to the match, of course, leaving the Newport star with no alternative other than to take a day's holiday.

Things worked very differently in the world of academia. Dennis Perrott was a lecturer at Cross Keys College which fell outside the Newport boundary and would not close its doors for the afternoon. Perrott enquired to his head of department what the procedure was regarding getting an afternoon off to play rugby and was told his request would have to be put in writing, the letter addressed to the college principal, no less. Pen was put to paper and the envelope forwarded to the top man, following which Perrott received a letter back requesting that he make an appointment to discuss the matter. All very formal, but that Dr Starkey was from Wolverhampton and known to be a lover of football does go some way to explaining the process the Newport wing now found himself caught up in.

At the appointed time Perrott presented himself at the principal's study and was asked to explain exactly what this was all about. It must have been similar to that old Bob Newhart skit, where Sir Walter Raleigh is trying to explain over the telephone what exactly tobacco was and why he had bought thousands of tons of the stuff. Starkey clearly had no idea what or who the All Blacks were, but permission was eventually granted with the proviso that this did not become a regular occurrence. Perrott was too polite to inform the man that New Zealand only visited once every ten years!

For David Jones there was to be no sympathetic nod from an understanding line manager. The simple question, could he have time off to play for Newport against New Zealand on Wednesday, got a simple answer, no! David Jones was a draughtsman at South Wales Switchgear in Pontllanfraith, and a short distance from Newbridge, home to one of the Valley clubs that liked to rough and tumble with Newport whenever the opportunity presented itself. The antipathy harboured by supporters of the Valley clubs toward Newport was well known, but this was an extreme reaction to a perfectly reasonable request. Whether Mr Alderson, the drawing office manager, was a supporter of the local club and enjoyed pulling rank or whether he was simply a stickler for the rules is long forgotten, but David Jones may not have played for Newport if fate had not taken a hand. His guardian angel came in the shape of a wisdom tooth, Mr Alderson's wisdom tooth, and the operation meant he was absent from work in the days leading up to the match. Jones had pretty much decided he was going to play and to hell with the consequences, but the production manager who replaced Alderson for a few days was happy to grant a leave of absence and David Jones caught the bus to Newport after putting in an appearance at work in the morning. What should have been a happy conclusion, with a straightforward example of common sense prevailing, became a storm in a teacup on Alderson's return. His authority had been undermined and he was far from happy about it. There were threats of Jones being sacked, such was the manager's anger, but that really would have been a case of bureaucracy gone mad and eventually peace was restored and life carried on.

It was on the bus from Pontllanfraith to Newport that the nerves set in, the stomach started to tighten up and Jones' first port of call on arrival at Newport bus station was the gents' toilet. Then it was a stop at the nearby Potter's Arms which, by then, was packed to the rafters with excited supporters but, making his way to the bar was a stroll in the park for the prop preparing to take on the might of the New Zealand front row. A schooner of sherry was the order of the day, great for settling the nerves with the added appeal of having no adverse effect on the bladder.

Glyn Davidge was another who enjoyed a sherry or two before a match. Some would say Glyn Davidge enjoyed much more than a sherry or two before a match, with gin known to be another favourite tipple of the Newport number eight. Rumours of sightings of Davidge in the King's Head Hotel and the front bar of the Royal Albert in the hours before kick-off abound, but wherever he settled to go through his pre-match ritual is irrelevant because Glyn Davidge was on the verge of rugby immortality, the legend of which would reach way beyond the history of Newport RFC. This was to be his day, the day the black and amber jersey, when removed, would reveal a body resembling the blue and black kit worn by great rivals Cardiff.

Then there were those who preferred a completely different preparation for the big occasion. Stuart Watkins arrived at the ground two or three hours before the kick-off but, even that early in the day, he was swept up by the crowd making their way to Rodney Parade from the other side of town. The roads from Chepstow and Caerleon were as busy as the short approach over the bridge from the town centre which did nothing to help calm the nerves and, when the new boy at the club finally pitched up in the home dressing room as the first player to arrive, it was his nerves that were winning the day. Time to sit down, relax, put things in perspective – it's only a game!

For those who had been around the block a few times, played on the bigger stage that is international rugby, the crowd of back-slapping supporters and well wishers encountered on the approach roads to Rodney Parade just added to what promised to be a grand day out. Brian Jones, Neville Johnson and Ian Ford had witnessed similar scenes on the day Newport played South Africa in 1961 when 20,000 spectators packed into the ground. But did they fill it?

Looking at Rodney Parade today, one sees a ground half of which is much as it always has been with the grandstand, enclosure and terrace behind the posts at the clubhouse end barely changed, while elsewhere there has been major redevelopment. Gone is the popular 'Bob Bank' on the Corporation Road side, replaced by seating for 2,000 spectators that runs the length of the pitch overlooked by private boxes and a dining facility. On the corner, at the old cricket pitch end, there are new changing rooms beneath a first-floor function suite which looks down on the playing field, together with two tiers of hospitality boxes which are positioned behind the dead-ball line. The capacity of this revamped Rodney Parade is now 9,092, a figure that makes it difficult for the modern-day rugby supporter to relate to the attendances seen in bygone years.

In March 1948, 22,000 spectators turned up to see Newport play Cardiff and, the following year, the same fixture attracted

24,500 through the turnstiles. In March 1951, once again, it was the intense rivalry between Newport and Cardiff and the crop of outstanding players representing the two clubs, that attracted the biggest attendance for a club match at Rodney Parade, when 27,000 enjoyed what was an all-ticket match. Later in the month, the Barbarians played in front of another all-ticket crowd, numbering 25,000, but it was January 1952 that saw the biggest attendance on record. This marked the visit of the fourth Springboks, when 32,000 were somehow shoehorned into every nook and cranny available. That will remain the biggest crowd ever to watch rugby football at Rodney Parade, but the 24,724 who witnessed Newport's finest hour would argue there wasn't room to swing a cat on the terraces, never mind accommodate another 7,000 among their number.

It goes without saying that the majority of those at the match were from Newport and its immediate environs, but there are many stories relating to others who had journeyed from further afield. Supporters are known to have poured into the town from the Valleys to the north and west, caught the local buses from Pontypool, Ebbw Vale etc. This was to be expected, but to make the trip from the Amman Valley in west Wales suggests an enthusiasm for the game rarely seen today, despite the improvements in transport networks. If you want to spend the best part of four hours travelling to see a game of rugby and then a similar time getting back to base, then that's fine, but to set off without match tickets in the hope of seeing a game known to be a sellout, well that has to be bordering on madness.

Unfazed by the real possibility of not getting into Rodney Parade, Howard Gabe Davies and Stewart Jones caught the bus for the hour-long journey to Swansea where they joined the London train that would stop at Newport. It was on the train that the gods shone down on these two determined young men, arriving in the guise of the local dentist who had acquired tickets through his father, the District F member of the WRU, and he just happened to have a spare pair of field tickets. They were in! They would be two of the 24,724. Since that day Gabe Davies has travelled the world following rugby, but the match that remains at the top of his list is the one that was played at Rodney Parade 50 years ago. Coming from a west Walian, that comment is indeed something for rugby supporters in Newport to savour, such is the rivalry between east and west Wales. West may conveniently rhyme with best, but it isn't necessarily true!

Not that the numbers meant anything in the aftermath of the match when every man and his dog claimed to have been in the ground. Must have been around 50,000 or 60,000 in there if all were to be believed and not only that, most of them would come out with the same old chestnut – know that photo of the drop goal? I could have taken that from where I was standing. The terracing behind the posts at the clubhouse end was certainly full, take it from one who was most definitely there, but ignore most of the subsequent claims. If a small percentage of those claiming to be in pole position are to be believed, Health and Safety would have had a field day.

Dick Uzzell was still enjoying his temporary residence at Caldicot and took the bus to Newport arriving in plenty of time to meet his sister who was travelling down from Birmingham by train. They had lunch in one of the Berni Steak Houses, where Uzzell was another to partake of a pre-match sherry. His sister did question whether he should be drinking alcohol before such an important game, but Uzzell explained that it was for medicinal purposes, having been told sherry was good for clearing the windpipes – believe that and you'll believe anything! True or not, here was another excuse to add to the list of benefits attributed to sherry, with only Davidge likely to have confirmed he had a few drinks before the match simply because he wanted to. Uzzell readily admits to having harboured some doubts regarding Newport's chances. He clearly didn't think his team could win, bearing in mind Newport's indifferent start to the season, what he witnessed at Oxford the previous week and an earlier encounter with the men in black.

Ten years had passed since an uncle took the eleven-year-old Dick Uzzell to Pontypool Park to see the 1953 tourists play the combined Pontypool & Cross Keys team. The famous bank at that park was no place for a schoolboy to get a good vantage point, but Uzzell's relative had come prepared and, with the benefit of a box to stand on, he was able to see the game. That New Zealand would win the match was never in doubt, but the young lad's abiding memory of the day was watching full-back Bob Scott practising his goal-kicking beforehand and landing long-distance goals with unerring accuracy – but in bare feet. Such displays of bravado are fine, but let's not get carried away. When push comes to shove, and the teams prepare to take the field, the bottom line tells us that it is 15 men against 15 men. That one team is kitted out in black jerseys, black shorts and black stockings with two white rings around the top and performs a dance before the game can get under way should count for nought, but it does. As the clock ticked down towards the kick-off, it is doubtful if Dick Uzzell was alone in expecting the worse, but such thoughts were best left unexpressed.

Fed and watered, Uzzell had an appointment to keep. He was in the team as selected, his name was in the morning's papers, and his name was against the number 13 jersey in the match-day programme. All well and good but late changes to published line-ups are common enough and Uzzell had to prove he was 100 per cent fit before the Newport selectors would let him take the field. There used to be a motor dealership occupying premises between Rodney Road and Rodney Parade on the approach to the ground, and it was there that Uzzell met Gerry Lewis and a local GP. In an office above the showroom, the doctor administered a pain-killing injection into the troublesome hamstring. Nothing underhand in that – injections often used to help a player manage any discomfort caused by a persistent injury, which in turn allowed him to get on with the job in hand. Now Uzzell had to convince the selectors that all was well. Once in the dressing room, Gerry Lewis confirmed there was no problem, that Uzzell was fit to play and, following a short display of stretching exercises, the centre could finally focus his mind on what lay ahead.

When Dick Uzzell set out for Newport on the morning of the match the Newport captain, Brian Price, stayed in Caldicot, preferring to gather his thoughts together in the solitude of his home. It had been a busy few months. He was appointed Newport captain in July, got married in August, moved to a new job and a new house in September, and if it were not for a game of rugby he would have been able to enjoy his 26th birthday in time-honoured fashion. Little did the Newport captain know that the best birthday gift he would ever receive was to be presented to him later in the day. Unlike some of the team, he had no problem getting the necessary time off work, the headmaster at Caldicot School found to be very accommodating. When the time came to set out for Newport, his route took him past the school where his wife Dorothy taught, and the children were waiting outside to give him a rousing send off. Such moments leave their own mark on the individual and each member of the Newport team would have experienced a similar moment on the morning of the match when, if it hadn't already, the penny would drop and the significance of the next few hours would finally register.

Bob Prosser may well have encountered Dick Uzzell at Newport railway station. The scrum-half was waiting for his father to arrive from Coventry, and the pair would then meet up with Prosser's uncle who was travelling down from the Rhondda. Birmingham, the Amman Valley, Coventry and the Rhondda Valley; and with the New Zealand High Commissioner arriving from London and the All Blacks from Porthcawl, all roads certainly did lead to Newport on that Wednesday.

Algy Thomas was another to benefit from a day off work. He was employed in the mining industry and the colliery manager was found to be most receptive to his situation when the request for leave of absence was received. If there were any traffic problems on route, Algy would have avoided them, his mode of transport a motorbike and for him it was straight to the ground, happy to pass the time in the dressing room with his mates as they arrived for the countdown.

Mates? Maybe not all of them. Algy Thomas and Glyn Davidge had a history that went back to Thomas's arrival at the club, and an incident that took place at a training session. It all started with a hard clip around the ear from behind. Then there was a second and soon after a third, by which time Thomas had worked out who was doing it and was not going to take any more. He grabbed hold of Davidge, got him in a head lock and had no intention of letting go. A body builder who had once been invited to take part in a Mr Universe contest, Algy Thomas had great upper body strength and could look after himself. With the other players gathered around, his demands for an apology fell on deaf ears – Davidge didn't apologise to anybody, but Thomas held firm. Insincere and begrudgingly given it might have been, but Thomas got what he wanted and life moved on, but these two were never destined to become great friends. Thomas was not alone in finding Glyn Davidge a difficult man to warm to, but Keith Poole experienced a different side to the number eight, recalling how Davidge took him under his wing when he first arrived at Rodney Parade. Differences aside, when it came to preparing to face New Zealand, the back row trio were going to have to work together, each had his individual role to play, but much more important to the cause was how they would function as a unit.

If the match had been played a year earlier, then the Newport back-row would have numbered 14, 15 and 16, but when those who make such decisions pronounced change, the revised formula saw the loose forwards allocated six, seven and eight with the reintroduction of number 13, which was worn by a centre. It was generally accepted that number seven would be the open-side wing forward with number six identifying the player packing down on the blind side of the scrum. Keith Poole's preferred position was open side but he would have to adapt if he wanted to secure his place in the Newport team. For whatever reason Poole had become attached to the number seven jersey, and when his selection was confirmed, he approached Thomas with a unusual request which Algy had no problem accommodating. On the day Poole would wear seven and, if Thomas's shock of fair hair wasn't enough to enable spectators to identify him, then it would be by the number six on his back.

The atmosphere in the home changing room was much as one would expect in the final minutes before the players made the walk down to the pitch. There were pre-match rituals to observe: Cheney would tie his boots and then go to great lengths cutting off the excess lace to ensure a smooth surface on the upper which would help his kicking routine; Davidge would spend a few minutes in the toilet throwing up; some players would talk for the sake of talking, something to help take their mind off the matter in hand; while for others silence was golden and they wouldn't utter a word.

The club had forked out for a new set of jerseys and shorts. Manufactured by Bukta, the kit was purchased from local sports outfitters Fussell's and, being new, had a good depth of colour which would gradually be lost once the washing machines got to grips with it. The famous black and amber tops, together with black shorts and the black stockings with two amber hoops around the top, was a striking combination of colour and style – a playing kit instantly recognised wherever rugby was played in Britain. Canterbury was not the global sportswear manufacturer known today but had been suppliers to the New Zealand RFU since time immemorial, and the All Blacks were kitted out in exactly that, barring the two white hoops at the top of the stockings.

The changing rooms were part of a block that included the clubhouse, gymnasium and offices. The two facilities enjoyed a common entrance before the home team would head upstairs and the visitors settle in below. Players would meet after the match in the communal shower room on the lower level but, until the referee knocked on the doors and asked the teams to make their way to the pitch, there would have been little or no contact between them. As the Newport players carefully made their way down the stairs, so did the visitors' changing room door open, and Keith Poole remembers being faced by a giant of a man who he understandably took to be a forward. Then he saw the number one on the jersey; this was Don Clarke, the full-back, for heaven's sake! What were the rest of them like? A few days earlier the baby of the Newport team hadn't heard of the All Blacks or the names of any of their star performers. This was his introduction to New Zealand rugby and he would never forget it. Game on!

CHAPTER SIX

All Black And Amber

"Singin' in the rain."
Arthur Freed (1894–1973)

T HE CHANGING ROOMS at Rodney Parade were a short walk from the pitch. The players, referee and touch judges would exit the building, walk across the tarmac that now covered the old cycle track and circled the tennis courts and bowling green, before jogging along the grass verge that led to the gated entrance found at the corner of the ground and the playing field beyond. If time permitted, there was an open area of grass often used for any last-minute preparations before the referee called the teams together at the gate and the visitors led the way down the short ramp and into the stadium proper. As the Newport and New Zealand players prepared to take the field, so did the rain start to fall. Nothing too heavy at first, just a persistent drizzle that was little more than an irritant but which steadily worked its way into a playing surface that had not dried out following the previous day's wet weather.

When Wilson Whineray led the All Blacks across the in-goal area, they received a rapturous welcome from the packed terraces and grandstand. Official figures confirmed that 24,724 spectators were in the ground, but it is certain the actual number present exceeds that, with many stories of people without tickets getting in by whatever means possible. The terracing behind the posts at the cricket pitch end was the most vulnerable, gatecrashers somehow clambering up the back of the elevated structure in their desperate attempts to claim a vantage point. There was no alternative for those desperate to see the match, the now all-too-familiar ticket touts still learning their trade in 1963, having only put a tentative toe in the water at international matches.

The rain was being driven across the ground by a south-westerly breeze. The Newport players would have it at their backs during the first half and were fully aware that they needed to take advantage of the elements while they were in their favour, get some valuable points on the board before the teams changed ends for the second period. The stage was set but, before Gwynne Walters could get the match under way, the New Zealand players lined up near the half-way line for the haka, the traditional Maori dance performed by the All Blacks at away matches.

Several versions of the haka have been used since the New Zealand Native team that toured Britain in 1888–9 first introduced it. It was a preamble to the game that quickly gained favour to such a degree that, if the haka was not performed, then part of the enjoyment gleaned from watching the All Blacks was missing, leaving spectators feeling short-changed. The 1905 tourists were accommodating, as were the Invincibles in 1924, but the third All Blacks dropped it from their repertoire before it was revived by Bob Stuart's men in 1953.

Of the different versions used the 'Ka Mate' haka became the one most associated with the All Blacks and it was this one that was performed at Rodney Parade by Wilson Whineray's team. Players were expected to treat the ritual with the greatest respect, and it would be some years before the spectacle was criticised for being too confrontational which, in turn, led to the opposition taking different slants on how it should be greeted. Indeed, in 1989, it was Newport captain Glen George who took his players to a spot under the posts where they grouped together, clearly refusing to take up the challenge. So incensed was All Black skipper Wayne 'Buck' Shelford, that he marched his troops up to the goal-line to confront the opposition. There was no contentious issue in 1963, the Newport players happy to get down on their haunches ten yards from the New Zealanders and embrace the moment.

Three players with Maori ancestry were among the 30-strong touring party and two of them played at Newport – Pat Walsh and Waka Nathan. The haka would be led by a Maori whenever possible, and it was the turn of Nathan to lay down the gauntlet, lead the players through the movements and chants. Fourteen players formed a line with Nathan taking up a slightly forward position at the end which enabled the team to follow his actions. Colin Meads had secured the position nearest to Nathan, from where the line moved away through Kel Tremain, Brian Lochore, the Clarke brothers and Ralph Caulton with vice-captain Kevin Briscoe, Bill Davis and Wilson Whineray at the far end.

You could have heard a pin drop as Waka Nathan gathered himself. The haka begins with the leader encouraging the players to slap their thighs, puff out their chests, bend the knees, follow with the hip and stomp their feet – 'Ringa pakia! Uma tiraha! Turi whatia! Hope whai ake! Waewae takahiakia kino!' As he warmed to his task, Nathan shouted 'Ka Mate, ka mate' (I die, I die) to which the team responds 'Ka ora, ka ora' (I live, I live). This is repeated before the players join together for the finale: 'Tenei te tangata puhuruhuru, Nana nei i tiki mai whakawhiti te ra, A Upane! Ka Upane!, A Upane Ka Upane, Whiti te ra!' (This is the hairy man who caused the sun to shine again for me. Up the ladder, up the ladder, up to the top. The sun shines!) – following which the team leap from the ground with arms held aloft and legs bent under them shouting 'Hi!' (Rise!).

The haka has changed. Now the whole squad of players takes to the field and line-up in ranks with the leader moving about them as he ups the ante. There is a lot of sticking out of tongues, actions suggesting the cutting of throats, and wide-eyed staring, which has prompted opponents to introduce a variety of ways of confronting the spectacle: form a wedge and walk towards it; refuse to move once the challenge has been laid down; seek out your opposite number and advance to within a couple of feet of him, get in his face; upset the All Blacks by asking them to vary the routine, which might see them perform the haka in the changing room; or you could just ignore it, kick a ball about until the whole thing was over.

Some may liken the haka of 50 years ago as being more akin to Morris dancing. Far from it. The intent in the players' eyes, the concentration on their faces as they went through the routine; these were men who demanded respect from the opposition and, on 30 October, the Newport team gave them that respect. But, when the players returned to ground following that final leap, so did that respect get put to one side. Newport had been correct in observing the ritual, nobody had put a foot out of line. Now there was only one way to ensure that these men in black and amber would get that respect fully reciprocated, and that was by beating the men in black.

The scoreboard positioned on the corner of the ground indicated that each half would be of 35 minutes duration, the normal playing time for club matches. With international opponents involved, this match was to be played over 80 minutes, another ten minutes for players to put their bodies on the line, get up and make another desperate tackle – all very demanding and a journey into the unknown for some. Rodney Parade was well equipped with floodlights and, with the skies darkening before the match got under way, spectators may well have expected these to be switched on before the final whistle. They would be disappointed. Agreement had been reached between the tourists and the home Unions clearly stating that no match or part of should be played under floodlights, ensuring that the forwards in particular would become hard to distinguish from one another as the clock ran down.

Despite the worsening weather, the match got under way at

a frenetic pace. New Zealand would play towards the cricket pitch in the first 40 minutes and it was Don Clarke who got proceedings under way, his placed kick-off directed to the left of the field and the packed terraces on the Corporation Road side of the ground. The All Black forwards reclaimed the ball and Briscoe sent a swift pass out to Kirton, which the outside-half was unable to gather. Keith Poole was first to the loose ball, with Bob Prosser ready to receive and weigh up the options. The scrum-half decided to run, moved to his left, spun the ball to Dennis Perrott, the left wing perfectly positioned to kick ahead and give chase. Corner flagging as all good number eight forwards should, Brian Lahore failed to claim the ball and knocked it back into the waiting arms of Don Clarke, who immediately kicked it into touch. It was a fast and furious opening minute that had seen play move across the width of the field and then taken deep into All Black territory. Twice in the opening salvo, New Zealand players were found wanting in the wet conditions. Twice the ball had gone to ground and twice the Newport forwards were there to pick up the pieces, hassle the opposition, lay down an early marker.

Newport had the throw-in at the first line-out and as the two sets of forwards prepared to compete for the ball, Perrott was the player who would throw it between them. This technique is now the responsibility of the hooker, which allows the wing to take up a defensive position if necessary or include himself in any complex plan of attack. There were no such routines for wing three-quarters to learn 50 years ago, but they were expected to deliver the ball to a nominated forward in the line-out with some degree of accuracy. The wing would take up a stance almost sideways on to the pitch, and deliver the ball with an over arm throw. The favoured targets were the big men in the second row, or those taking up position at the tail of the line-out. In Brian Price, Newport had one of the game's great exponents of the line-out. The captain would leap from the ground to claim the ball with seeming ease, so accomplished was he in this particular facet of play. This, at a time when jumpers had to get off the ground unassisted, and were subjected to much unwanted attention from their opposite number as the ball was claimed and a smooth return to terra firma negotiated.

As the game began to unfold, so too did it become apparent that the Newport forwards were proving to be more than equal to the task before them. They certainly weren't going to struggle in the set pieces which one might have expected, neither were they being outplayed in the loose. The front row was functioning well in the scrum, Price and Ian Ford were looking composed and the loose forwards were everywhere. Algy Thomas and Keith Poole would have covered every blade of grass come the final whistle and Glyn Davidge was causing mayhem when the ball was on the ground, the number eight putting together what would be his finest performance on a rugby pitch. Clearly happy with the early exchanges, the Newport captain was quick to gather his forwards round and pass on his initial thoughts – we can hold them up front but we must keep our discipline.

Discipline. When it came down to discipline in the opening quarter, it was the All Blacks who were getting on the wrong side of Mr Walters. Twice in the first ten minutes Ray Cheney was given opportunities to open the scoring, both kicks at goal from wide out on the left-hand side of the field. The first, an effort from 45 yards, wandered off course at the last moment, before a longer kick, measuring all of 55 yards, failed to threaten the posts. When the shrill whistle announced another serious infringement at a line-out, Cheney prepared to take his third kick at goal, once again from near the left touchline and another that would have to travel 45 yards plus, straight and true. This attempt drifted left of the posts, the ball went dead and it was for Don Clarke to get the match restarted with a drop-out from the 25-yard line.

Clarke's drop kick set in motion the most memorable 60 seconds ever witnessed at Rodney Parade. It wasn't the prettiest passage of play seen at the ground – there have been hundreds upon hundreds of more entertaining moments to recall – but it was the most dramatic: it was the most thrilling; it was the most exhilarating; it was the most heart-warming; it was the most uplifting and it would become the most talked about. It may well have been a little untidy as it arrived at its denouement but, as periods of 60 seconds go, then this was as good as it gets. The most perfect minute that has ever passed at Rodney Parade and so it will always be.

With his forwards taking position on the left, Clarke looked to be readying himself to put the ball up for them to contest. With a last moment change of mind, the full-back elected to go right and a long drop-out saw the ball bounce into touch between the halfway line and the Newport ten-yard line on the grandstand side of the ground. Perrott wiped the wet ball, received his instructions and prepared himself. He mentally measured the trajectory the ball would take to the appointed receiver and launched it on its way. It was long. In the wet, unpredictable conditions, Dennis Perrott threw the ball to the tail of the line-out where, on such a wet day, pretty much anything could happen to it. Waiting to get his hands on the leather missile was Davidge who collected it before being collared by the All Black loose forwards and taken to ground. Coming round from the front of the line-out, Graham Bevan went to Davidge's assistance, grabbing the ball before turning to feed the waiting Bob Prosser. The scrum-half took the briefest of moments to weigh up the options, then executed a perfect dive pass sending the ball into the waiting hands of David Watkins.

Following a recent match, the outside-half had received a deserved reprimand from Bryn Meredith after fooling around inside the 25 before attempting a clearance kick that was charged down and a try scored. Meredith was not happy, and the few words he had addressed to Watkins in the interim were far from complimentary. Watkins could be the most frustrating player to accommodate but, at his best, he was pure genius. Receiving the ball from Prosser, the outside-half had three options available to him – pass to the waiting Brian Jones, kick for the corner or run. Watkins decided to run.

The outside-half set off on a path that took him beyond the reach of the fast-approaching New Zealand forwards and targeted a gap he had identified between the two centres. Did he find it? Was there enough room to escape the outstretched arms and hands trying to get a grip on his slight frame? Knowing Brian Jones had moved left and taken up position inside him and that Dick Uzzell was to his right if anything went wrong, Watkins went for broke. Ian MacRae over-committed himself in anticipation of a pass and Pat Walsh was simply too slow. Only Ralph Caulton responded quickly to the danger but all the wing could do was move infield, take Dick Uzzell with him and hope that by crowding Watkins he would be forced to kick the ball. With his opposite number drawn away from the touchline, Stuart Watkins now found himself with room to take play forward if the ball were to come his way. The outside-half may well have considered passing to Uzzell, but the brief moment that might have allowed him to do so had gone. The centre was up alongside him and with Caulton now little more than an arm's length away, he was rapidly running out of options. Somehow David Watkins got a pass out to Stuart Watkins, before he was brought to ground by Walsh who had taken the most direct route to Watkins' curved run, while behind them Dick Uzzell continued to make his way upfield, now heading towards a position left of the posts.

When Stuart Watkins received the ball he had time to make three long strides before the covering figure of Kel Tremain came into his peripheral vision. Watkins would later remark that Tremain was the most perfect specimen he ever saw on a rugby field, but this was not the time to be dwelling on that. He was going to be caught, he knew it and Stuart Watkins decided the only way to continue what looked to be a promising attack was to get the ball back into the middle of the field; so he launched a mighty cross-kick which came down ten yards in front of the posts. The cross kick is rarely seen in the modern game, but in 1963 it was an essential part of any self-respecting wing three-quarter's armoury. It was a given that, as the ball was being moved through the hands, spun out wide to the wings, the forwards would gravitate to the middle of the field and head in the direction of the opposition goal line ready to contest any kicks that may be lofted high in their direction. Which is exactly what happened following Stuart Watkins' effort.

Brian Lochore failed to gather the ball at the first attempt, giving the advancing Newport forwards sufficient time to lay claim to it. Prominent among them were Ian Ford and Neville Johnson, with Poole and David Jones in support to feed off any scraps. It was all very untidy, with the ball looking to come back on the New Zealand side of the ruck before it bobbed up in front of Jones who had the vision to release it to Bob Prosser and let the scrum-half make the decision as to what happened next. Prosser looked to his left where the black and amber jerseys appeared to outnumber the black ones. He took a couple of quick steps and, with his outside-half partner not yet back in position, passed to Dick Uzzell, the centre having continued his run upfield.

Was it a moment's indecision? Did Dick Uzzell know that somewhere out to his left Dennis Perrott was screaming for the ball? For the briefest of seconds the wing had what appeared to be a clear run to the line, but Uzzell elected to step back inside where the defenders were moving in on him. The anguish and disbelief seen on the faces of the Newport players nearest to Uzzell was as nothing when they realised that the centre was intent on dropping for goal. Dick Uzzell drop a goal?... unheard of. But Uzzell did drop for goal. The centre swung his right leg and the two essential components of any successful kick at the posts fell into place; the ball set off in the right direction and it was high enough to get over the crossbar – just. A scrappy affair it most certainly was, but Newport had opened the scoring in the 15th minute of a match in which they were looking the better team. Now that superiority was reflected on the scoreboard – 3–0.

Across the river in the town's reference library, which was once found on Lower Dock Street, the signs requesting 'silence' were being strictly observed. Students and researchers were gathering information for whatever purpose when the tranquility of academia was rudely interrupted by a loud roar. Studying for a university exam, Clive Wood recalls the bemused looks on the faces of those lost in their thoughts, nobody able to identify what had rudely interrupted the grey matter as it set about its business. Of course, this being approximately 3.15 p.m. the cheers of the crowd following Dick Uzzell's drop goal were carried from Rodney Parade on the back of the prevailing wind, crossing the river and dispersing around the town impacting on the library en route. No sooner had it arrived than it was gone, and it would be another 70 minutes before a similar outburst would be released.

The All Blacks had enjoyed very little territorial advantage in the first quarter and, with this in mind, Don Clarke decided to place his restart deep into the Newport half of the field. The ball rolled into the in-goal area, was touched down and passed to Brian Jones who would take the restart. Appreciating the importance of immediately taking play back into the New Zealand half, Jones kicked long. Clarke collected in front of the posts but failed to find touch, the ball falling into the waiting arms of Ian Ford who had positioned himself close to the right touchline in anticipation of a more orthodox restart by the Newport centre.

Ian Ford was the oldest player on the field. At 34 years of age he was two years older than Ian Clarke, the elder statesman of the All Blacks, and less than twelve months younger than the referee. This was his 15th season at Rodney Parade and he had recently become the first Newport player to reach 400 appearances for the club. A few years earlier there had been murmurings on the terraces that the second-row forward was past his best, but he was currently enjoying a purple patch in his long career and would play on for another two seasons. But did you really want an ageing second-row forward fielding a high ball deep inside his own half with the rain coming down and the might of New Zealand rugby approaching with a head of steam up? Ian Ford would probably not have been most spectators' first choice in such a situation, but what he did could not have been bettered. Ford collected the ball near the touchline, took a few steps forward and launched the most perfect kick deep into New Zealand territory which sent Don Clarke covering back. Not content with having disposed of the ball in fine fashion, Ford then set off in chase and was up on the full-back before Clarke could compose himself and the clearance kick was scrambled away to give Newport the put-in at a line-out between the 25 and half-way line.

The effort from the Newport forwards in the early exchanges was extraordinary, the much lauded New Zealand eight having to play second fiddle to their opposite numbers. Brian Price dominated the middle of the line-out and the back row secured any ball that was thrown long. The front row were proving superior in the set pieces and, at the final reckoning, hooker Graham Bevan would be credited with five strikes against the head, with two claimed by his opposite number. The Newport back row were making life difficult for the New Zealand half-backs and Davidge was killing any loose ball he could get his hands on before a concerted attack could develop. The New Zealand backs had few enough opportunities in the first 40 minutes but when a half chance presented itself there was a black and amber jersey on hand to force the play which generally produced a hastily dispatched kick to the touchline.

With six minutes of the half remaining, New Zealand had their best territorial position of the half, a scrum set in the middle of the field 15 yards inside the Newport half. A quick heel was gathered up by Briscoe and the scrum-half broke away before passing to Earle Kirton. The outside-half took play on, but the timing of his pass to MacRae was misjudged, the centre receiving the ball at the same moment Brian Jones and Dick

Uzzell arrived, the centres bringing him to ground and the ball falling loose. Enter Stuart Watkins, he of the football skills, the would-be centre-forward. The wing kicked the ball on; chased it and kicked it on again; caught up with it and kicked it on again by which time Watkins was little more than ten yards from the New Zealand posts. Realising the danger, Bill Davis had covered back from his position out on the right flank and bravely fell on the ball. Watkins was joined by Poole and the pair secured possession, the wing forward breaking left before passing to Graham Bevan who could not hold on to the wet ball. Bevan hadn't knocked on, the ball falling behind him allowing the arriving Newport forwards time to claim it and recycle to Prosser. In those brief moments the New Zealand defence had reorganised and when David Watkins received a pass from the scrum-half, there were few options available to him. An expert drop kicker, Watkins fired the ball in the direction of the posts, but it sailed wide and with it went the chance of an all-important second score.

After 35 minutes of increasingly heavy rain and with 30 players showing no regard for it, the pitch was beginning to cut up, with parts looking decidedly the worse for wear. Not quite a ploughed field, but maybe a quagmire – soft and sticky. Newport had played Wasps on Saturday and, much to the annoyance of head groundsman Fred Cox, training sessions were also held on it on Monday and Tuesday. Whether the poor conditions underfoot would favour one side above the other is debatable, but what they did suggest was that, with the rain unlikely to let up, this was going to be a low-scoring match and with every minute that ticked by those three points on the board were looking more and more valuable.

Newport's main objective was to deny Don Clarke any kicks at goal. How he would have fared on the slippery surface we shall never know, but when Waka Nathan was caught off-side at a scrum, Ray Cheney prepared to take his fourth penalty. The first three had all been on the left of the field; now he would have a shot from the right, but still from a distance of

50 yards. None of the four kicks would have been easy in fine conditions, but with the ball wet and heavy and the surface underfoot not lending itself to a firm stance at the moment of contact, Cheney had little in his favour other than a following breeze. This attempt was both wide and short, but it ensured that another minute was run down and that New Zealand would spend the next preparing for the line-out that would follow Clarke's kick to touch. The final act of an enthralling first half saw New Zealand take play into Newport territory. A long kick ahead was fielded by Cheney inside the 25, the full-back calmly sidestepping the advancing Bill Davis before kicking the ball into the grandstand, allowing Gwynne Walters to call a temporary halt to proceedings.

There would be no rapid retreat from the field. No ten minutes respite in the warmth of a changing room listening to others confirm what had gone right and what was going wrong – no tactical appraisal to suffer. And there would be no threat of being substituted. Barring injury or dismissal, the same 15 players would see out the match. The only comfort enjoyed in the five-minute break came from an orange segment which would be sucked dry before the teams changed ends in readiness for the resumption of play.

It had long been the general consensus on the terraces that Newport was a better team in the second half of a game if playing towards the clubhouse end of the field, playing towards the beer! That would not be the case today, as Ray Cheney took the restart and sent a long kick deep into New Zealand territory forcing a clearance which led to a line-out on the 25-yard line. With both teams looking for that early advantage, play moved up and down the Corporation Road side of the pitch with a series of line-outs dominating the early exchanges. The match had been played in good spirits, with no quarter asked and none given. Only once did any player look like taking another to task, when Neville Johnson reacted to something Colin Meads might have said or done, but this only extended to a bit of serious eyeballing before Whineray pulled his player away and the moment was immediately defused.

It was clear from the outset of the second half that New Zealand were going about their business with greater purpose than seen in the first 40 minutes. With the benefit of the breeze now at their backs, this would be put to good use as the half unfolded. Two aspects of their game in particular were being introduced at every opportunity. Firstly, Whineray regularly led a charge from the back of a line-out whenever the ball was presented to him and secondly, Don Clarke would enter the three-quarter line when the All Black forwards won good possession from the set pieces. This was a dangerous ploy, and the Newport defence would be called upon time and again to stop the big man before he could get into his stride.

Rugby union has changed considerably since the 1960s. Looking at footage of matches played 50 years ago, the most noticeable difference is not that seen by any changes to the laws: the ability to kick direct to touch from anywhere on the field for example, or that a penalty kick put out of play would see the throw-in at the resultant line-out pass to the offending team. These are among numerous modifications, but what stands out above all else is the ability of the front rows and the five forwards behind them to get down quickly at the formation of the scrum, allowing the game to restart without any protracted arm wrestle. To watch Johnson, Bevan and Jones face Whineray, Major and Clarke before the six men locked arms and got on with things, poses many questions about the most contentious part of the modern game. But get on with it they did and, no sooner had the ball been won than the tight forwards were up and heading for the next breakdown.

The match could never be called a game of two halves, but the All Blacks looked a different team after the interval. There were moments when Newport put the visitors under pressure, created phases that took play deep into New Zealand territory, but the players were unable to capitalise on it. A clever kick into the left corner by David Watkins gave Perrott a glimmer of hope as he followed up and caught the retreating Davis in possession, but desperate New Zealand hands retrieved the ball and it was kicked to the safety of the terraces. It was during this third quarter that Gerry Lewis came into his own. Firstly, Algy Thomas was in need of running repairs to a head wound before an unholy quiet descended across Rodney Parade as the spectators saw Davidge lying prone on the ground. While Thomas and Poole were performing great deeds in the open, tackling like dervishes to snuff out any attack before it became a threat, Davidge had been getting to know the nether regions of the All Black forwards, as time and again they set about trying to dislodge the ball from his grasp as he was quite legitimately killing it on the ground. He wouldn't get away with it today, but in 1963 this was within the laws of the game, as was the All Blacks right to try and extricate the ball by the use of some deft footwork. Davidge's bruised body would take time to recover, but the short-term problem attended to by Lewis appeared to be concussion. Davidge was freshened up, the fingers were counted and he was allowed to return to the fray as Gerry Lewis and his magic sponge, the two unsung heroes of Newport's famous victory, made for the touchline.

Knowing time was running out, New Zealand started to open up, take more chances in an attempt to gain territorial advantage, create the pressure that would see the home team give away penalties at the very least – penalties which the best goal kicker in world rugby would convert to salvage a draw or better. A clean take at a line-out on halfway saw the ball swiftly moved to midfield, to Pat Walsh who was collared by Dick Uzzell and Algy Thomas before the centre had a chance to take play over the advantage line. With the forwards arriving as one, the ruck that followed the breakdown could have been blown up for any number of infringements but, when the whistle went, it was in Newport's favour.

"Off-side!" The dulcet tones of referee Walters rang out

and Brian Price called up Ray Cheney for what would be his fifth kick at goal. He would have to wait as Algy Thomas was receiving more attention but, with the running repairs completed and Gerry Lewis scuttling off the pitch, once again the Newport full-back sized up the task in hand. This kick would be attempted from a point between the half-way line and the New Zealand ten-yard line. Yet another kick from over 45 yards that may have been straight in front of the posts, but was also directly into the wind and rain. Cheney had no success with his place kicking during the course of the match but, with all five kicks at goal ranging between 45 and 55 yards, combined with the slippery surface, the unfavourable elements and the occasion, the full-back can be excused. The fifth attempt was Cheney's best effort, the ball hitting the crossbar at the junction with the upright before bouncing back into play and creating a moment's panic among the onlooking All Blacks who failed to gather it cleanly, a knock-on giving Newport a scrum in front of the posts. What a great place to be with only ten minutes remaining on the clock. This was drop goal territory and, when he received the ball from the diving Prosser, David Watkins had already decided what he was going to do. He took up position to the right of the posts, within comfortable range for someone of his undoubted ability. A shimmy to the right, a quick look at the target, take aim and kick, but for the second time, he could only watch on as his effort swung away to the left.

Another long restart by Clarke returned play deep into the Newport half. Cheney gathered and put the ball out in front of the grandstand, but an All Black infringement at the following line-out conceded a penalty. Bob Prosser reacted immediately, grabbed the ball and elected to run straight at the slowly retreating All Blacks, thereby gaining a further ten yards. The play was getting more frenzied, both sides aware time was running out. Could Newport hold on to the slender lead or would the All Blacks create something that would spoil the day? Benefiting from the extra ten yards, Cheney's touch finder took the home side back into New Zealand territory and from the set piece, a clever kick by Watkins rolled into touch at the corner flag.

Was it five minutes remaining on the clock or six? How much injury time would there be? The 15 Newport heroes needed some help. They had given their all, now it was time for the 16th man to take over. From the depths of the packed ground what started with a lone voice was instantly taken up by the other 24,723 spectators officially present plus a few others. They chose 'Bread of Heaven', that stirring hymn so popular with the crowd at international matches in Cardiff. But this wasn't a chorus inspired by a recording played over the speaker system. This was the real thing, a wonderful rendition of a melody and words that soared out from the packed terraces and grandstand, words everyone is familiar with... "Bread of Heaven, Bread of Heaven, Feed Me Till I Want No More". It can send shivers down the spine, cause the hair on arms to bristle, make one feel good. And that is if you are in the crowd, goodness knows what impact it has when you are preparing for a line-out a couple of yards from the New Zealand line.

It was a messy affair that resulted in a Newport scrum. The ball was won but the home pack were in retreat and the maul that developed led to the only serious mistake David Watkins made during the 80 minutes. In fairness, the outside-half appeared to have slipped on the wet surface, but he should have settled for putting the ball straight out of play rather than take a few unnecessary steps. They had him. The New Zealand forwards had Watkins. They got the ball, they moved away from the breakdown and headed off towards the Newport line with the greatest intent – men on a mission. It would likely be their last opportunity to salvage something from the game and they knew it. Tremain, Major and Nathan rumbled deep into the 25 before the movement was brought to an end by a loose kick to touch. The All Blacks claimed the ball at the line-out and Briscoe set Kirton on his way. Don Clarke made another foray into the line, but when the ball reached Bill Davis, the right wing had little choice other than to kick for the corner where the waiting Cheney gathered and ran into touch.

Breathtaking stuff if you were a New Zealand supporter, potentially heartbreaking if you weren't. This was the period of most concerted pressure Newport had allowed New Zealand to enjoy over the preceding 78 minutes. There was another line-out to contest. It would almost certainly be the last one of the match and, if it were lost, then enough time remained on the clock to turn the match on its head. It was lost. New Zealand claimed the ball at the tail, Nathan making a determined charge for the Newport posts, ably supported by Horsley and Tremain. The defence held firm before a knock-on brought play to a halt. Scrum. New Zealand ball. What to do? A scrum in front of the posts with a New Zealand put-in suggests a penalty kick waiting to happen.

Earle Kirton took up position behind the set piece, with Don Clarke a couple of yards further back. The scrum being set in the middle of the field made it difficult to defend with the New Zealand backs positioned to left and right of the outside-half. Options galore, with Clarke well positioned for an attempt at a drop goal. Whatever followed it was certain to be the final play of the match. The Newport players had prepared for pretty much every eventuality, spent hours on the training ground rehearsing the tactics and moves that had all been executed with barely a hitch: kick for the corners, keep Clarke on the back foot, maintain the highest standard of discipline. Whether the players were primed to defend a three-point lead at an opposition scrum in front of their posts in injury time was another matter. In the modern game New Zealand would go in search of a penalty or even better a penalty try, as would any other team. That is the mentality now threatening the game of rugby football, but 50 years ago their predecessors approached such situations with a very different mind-set.

John Major heeled swiftly and the second-row forwards guided the ball back to the feet of Brian Lochore who allowed it to pass into the hands of Kevin Briscoe, the scrum-half mentally prepared to go right. When he made his move, Briscoe took Kirton and the looming figure of Don Clarke with him. The ball was spun through the hands by Kirton, then Clarke, who for the briefest of moments looked as if he had doubled in size. A man-mountain on the run, seeking out a gap that wasn't there before Dennis Perrott put in a tackle and the full-back decided it was time to release Bill Davis, put the wing in at the corner flag and take his chance with the conversion. The wing might well have scored if not for the speed and accuracy with which Algy Thomas flung himself at Davis, collaring him in an all-embracing tackle that took both players into touch. Gwynne Walters blew his whistle but this blast was a bit different, it didn't signal another line-out but full-time. The match was over. Newport had achieved what most forecasters had considered impossible. The club had claimed the scalp of the most lauded of the southern hemisphere nations, a victory to add to those over South Africa in 1912 and Australia in 1957.

At the fifth attempt Newport had defeated the mighty New Zealand All Blacks. The magnitude of the achievement would not be fully appreciated for some months but, for now, the players could enjoy the moment, congratulate each other and commiserate with the vanquished. As hundreds of supporters climbed the surrounding fencing and ran on to the pitch, both teams would have appreciated that play came to an end at the corner where they had entered the arena 90 minutes earlier. A rapid exit beckoned, but the excited supporters were not going to let their heroes get off so lightly. It proved to be a long walk back to the changing rooms, the Newport players met by crowds of supporters wanting to shake a hand, give a congratulatory slap on the back, try and grab an autograph. A real 'I was there' moment, long before 'I was there' moments were recognised.

It took longer than usual but, eventually, the Newport team claimed the sanctuary of the changing room. One by one they climbed the stairs, each longing for the moment when they could rest their exhausted bodies, grab a seat before heading back down for a much needed shower. Joining the players in the changing room were committee men, VIPs, representatives of the press and the men who had helped mastermind the All Blacks' downfall – Bryn Meredith, Ian MacJennett and Bryn Williams. It was chaotic, and at first nobody noticed the door had opened and a man in a white sweater was standing there waiting for an opportunity to say a few words. Was it Brian Jones or Brian Price who first saw him and called for silence? Either way, a hush fell over the room as Wilson Whineray spoke. He congratulated Newport on a fine victory, confirmed that the All Blacks had been beaten by a better side on the day and, as a parting shot, Whineray expressed the wish that the players would be selected en block by the Welsh selectors, enabling New Zealand another crack at them. And then he was gone with renditions of "For he's a jolly good fellow..." following him down the stairs.

By now thousands of supporters had gathered outside the building and were clearly not going to disperse until they had given the players a final send off. The windows of the changing room overlooked a flat roof of some size, and it was here that Brian Price led his team to acknowledge the well-wishers. The windows were swung open and the players stepped out on to the roof to tumultuous applause. The rain was still falling, but it made little impression on those below and the cheers showed no sign of letting up. This was a great moment, and many from the Newport team would recall those minutes spent on the roof as their favourite memory of the day. Then it was back into the changing room and down to the showers. They would join the All Blacks for a meal before heading to the clubhouse and the adjoining gymnasium, the venue for a dance which would get under way later in the evening. It promised to be a long night.

Immediate reaction to the match was unanimous in deciding that the better side had won. New Zealand manager Frank

Kilby was generous in defeat: "It was Newport all the way. They were the better side and we did not look like scoring. Our boys were not good enough but we have no excuses or complaints. Congratulations to the Newport club."

Don Clarke was full of praise for Dick Uzzell's winning score and, in a quiet moment, confided to Ray Cheney that he had not envied the full-back having to take five long penalties in such poor conditions. Clarke had enjoyed better afternoons on a rugby field, but some years later he would confirm that the only match in his playing career in which he did not have a single kick at goal was against Newport at Rodney Parade. Having had time to gather his thoughts Wilson Whineray commented, "We have learnt something from this defeat and we shall work on our weaknesses. Don't forget, Newport never crossed our line, so our lads couldn't have done too badly. The crowd also helped – but on the day Newport certainly deserved to win."

Travelling with the All Blacks, New Zealand rugby correspondent Terry McLean wrote: "The plain, inescapable and immutable fact about this most thrilling game was that the better team won – and after all, no one can possibly complain at this very proper conclusion to a sporting encounter. I myself would have put the margin of superiority at higher than three points for one specially significant reason – not in all the one hundred or more games I have seen All Black teams play in the last ten or fifteen years have I seen a representative forward pack from New Zealand so thoroughly well contained as was Wilson Whineray's team."

To the victors the spoils, but equally magnanimous was Newport captain, Brian Price. "They have not settled down yet. It was only their third game. I suppose we were lucky to play them so early in their tour but they are going to get much better." When asked about his team and individual performances, Price confirmed what was the general consensus of opinion. "If anyone has to be singled out for special mention it has to be Glyn Davidge. He fell on the ball so many times the New Zealanders must have thought there were three of him."

Davidge was full of praise for Keith Poole, while Ray Cheney confirmed it was the most exciting game he had ever played in. The full-back was convinced his final kick at goal was heading over the crossbar and was celebrating four feet in the air when the ball bounced back into play. Bob Prosser rated the forward display as "...the best I have seen from our pack. They gave me plenty of protection, plenty of the ball and plenty of confidence." David Watkins confessed to being "...nervous at the start. But like Brian Price said when we lined up against them – they only had 15 men the same as us. Now I hope I don't wake up in the morning and find it was all a dream!"

For Brian Jones the victory ended a ten-year wait and completed a notable hat-trick. BJ was in the team defeated by the All Blacks in January 1954, since when he had played in the side that defeated Australia in 1957 and represented the Barbarians when that famous club inflicted the only defeat on the fifth Springboks in the final match of their tour in 1961. Another ready to recognise the outstanding performance by the Newport pack, Jones highlighted the contribution made by the front row, "Graham Bevan was a grand hooker and Nev Johnson and David Jones were superb props".

Away from the match and all the praise heaped on the Newport players individually or as a collective, one fact stands out above all others: Ray Cheney, Stuart Watkins, Dick Uzzell, Brian Jones, Dennis Perrott, David Watkins, Bob Prosser, Neville Johnson, Graham Bevan, David Jones, Brian Price, Ian Ford, Algy Thomas, Keith Poole and Glyn Davidge had not previously played together as a team when they took the field against New Zealand.

This is unusual in itself but what completes a remarkable piece of rugby trivia is that Ray Cheney, Stuart Watkins, Dick Uzzell, Brian Jones, Dennis Perrott, David Watkins, Bob

Prosser, Neville Johnson, Graham Bevan, David Jones, Brian Price, Ian Ford, Algy Thomas, Keith Poole and Glyn Davidge never played together again. When Newport RFC defeated New Zealand on that most famous day in its long history, it proved to be the only match in which the 15 players enjoyed each other's company – extraordinary!

CHAPTER SEVEN

Men of the Moment

"Success is a science;
if you have the conditions you get the result."
Oscar Wilde (1854–1900)

THE CELEBRATIONS WENT on long into the night but, after spending a couple of hours with the Newport players and mingling among the supporters in the clubhouse, the All Blacks boarded their coach for the journey back to Porthcawl. To have suffered defeat so early in the tour must have been a huge disappointment, but the players and management were more than generous with their congratulations and praise. Any aspirations of invincibility had been left on the playing field and the tourists departed Rodney Parade with their respect intact knowing there were another 33 matches to be played in which to diminish the impact of one defeat. As the coach made its way through Newport, the passengers would have seen carousing supporters, helping each other along the way from public house to public house. Maybe one would break away from his mates to demonstrate how the winning score had come about, stand on one decidedly shaky leg while swinging the other in tribute to Dick Uzzell. And what of the Newport hero? What can one do to top what would always be the finest moment in a rugby career that had barely started? How about getting arrested, crossing the long arm of the law and being carted off to the local nick for the night. Why not give that a try?

There were a lot of disgruntled people in the clubhouse at Rodney Parade when the announcement was made that the pumps were running dry, the last barrels had been connected and the draught ale drinkers were on borrowed time. This was always likely to happen after such an afternoon, but maybe not quite so early in the evening. Help was needed and in 'Bunner' Travers the club was able to call on someone who knew someone, who knew someone, who knew someone etc. Travers was a former Welsh international hooker of some renown who had the rare distinction of playing for Wales before and after the Second World War but, of more immediate importance, he was also the licensee of a public house in Pill, an area of Newport near the thriving docks and, as such, the home of many popular drinking houses. So Bunner knew someone who knew someone, who knew someone and he set off in a Land Rover driven by Ian Ford to tap up his numerous contacts in the licensing trade before returning with a vehicle full of bottles of beer to replenish the rapidly disappearing stock.

In the meantime, there was a danger that valuable drinking time could be lost and that a short-term alternative should be found. The common consensus is that Ray Cheney was the instigator, Brian Jones and Dick Uzzell among the players who followed his lead. Off they went, over the bridge before heading down Dock Street, past the bus station and into The Potters Arms which had certainly not run out of beer. The place was packed, but the crowd made way for the new arrivals and it was as the parting of the Red Sea when Cheney and company made their way to the bar. Did they have to buy their drinks? Doubtful, but drinks they had and when it came time to leave, make their way back to the club for the dance that was by now well under way, Dick Uzzell decided to help himself to a souvenir. At the end of the bar stood a soda syphon. Not the sort of item you could put in your pocket or discreetly hide under a coat, but one which caught Uzzell's attention and he walked out of The Potters Arms with it held aloft.

Now soda syphons are useful things. Point them at a glass

of whisky, press the nozzle and a flow of carbonated water tops up the glass to the desired level. Uzzell's demands on the glass cylinder reached no further than a friendly squirt at his mates who all took it in good spirit. Fine. But when Dick Uzzell decided to aim the thing at Police Constable 123 who had just walked into their path and give the unsuspecting officer of the law a good dousing, he was in trouble. There was no doubt the policeman was intent on making an example of what he perceived to be one of the Newport supporters – after all, they were going to make his night on the beat a busy one. It took a lot of persuading, but eventually the upholder of law and order was convinced that his collar was none other than Dick Uzzell, the player who only a few hours earlier had scored the points that secured Newport's famous victory. The reprimand was severe, extreme in the utmost. Any further nonsense and he would not be so lenient, but he let the players go on their way and Dick Uzzell remained a free man. There would be no night spent behind bars before joining any other miscreants hauled before the local magistrate the next morning. Now that would have been a story!

The Welsh public at large were able to read about the match in Thursday's edition of the *Western Mail*, the national newspaper of Wales renowned for its coverage of rugby by correspondents JBG Thomas and John Billot. The match report filled the back page of the broadsheet under JBG's wonderful headline NOW IS THEIR HOUR... subbed by, 'All Blacks' Power Play Spiked by Men of Gwent – Uzzell Goal Decisive'. The main photograph captured the moment when David Watkins broke through the New Zealand defence. The montage included a shot of Stuart Watkins launching his cross kick and another showing the Newport forwards as they competed for the ball in front of the posts. The extended coverage of the match also included a photograph of the moment the players came out of the changing room and onto the flat roof to receive the applause of those gathered below.

The vital moment was not included but a photograph

showing Dick Uzzell's drop goal as it clears the crossbar does exist. This is believed to have been taken by a staff photographer on a Swansea newspaper, *The Evening Post*, who arrived late at the ground and was perfectly positioned behind the posts to record the decisive moment. It clearly shows the ball passing over the crossbar with a couple of feet to spare, unlike a painting later commissioned by the club which employs artistic licence to give the impression the ball sailed high between the posts.

Later in the day the Newport-based *South Wales Argus* headlined 'NEWPORT COMPLETE THE HAT-TRICK – Great Pack Subdue the All Blacks'. Rugby correspondent, Jack Davis, explored the suggestion that the Newport pack had played as the All Blacks themselves like to, and what an achievement it was to beat them at their own game. Davis also reported how the New Zealand High Commissioner, speaking after the match, confirmed that he would be sending immigration papers to David Watkins!

Word of Newport's victory reached the four corners of the land courtesy of the national press, and wherever the All Blacks were scheduled to play a degree of optimism entered the equation. Newport had proved Wilson Whineray's fifth All Blacks could be beaten. Was there another team capable of claiming the most famous scalp in world rugby? Only time would tell, but for now it was back to the training paddock for the vanquished and back to work for the victors, or for Dick Uzzell, back to college.

If not for his new-found fame. Dick Uzzell might have been able to reintegrate himself into the college routine without any questions being asked following what was now an extended absence. He insists that reports in the press telling of family illness and his desire to be at his father's side are completely unfounded, but they had muddied the waters and when he arrived back at St Luke's on Thursday the first thing drawn to his attention was a sign on the notice board which read Dick Uzzell 3 New Zealand 0 next to which was a message asking him to report to the principal. It was with mixed feelings that he made his way to the secretary's office, from where he was immediately ushered in to the inner sanctum. "Would you like a sherry?" were the first words uttered and Uzzell knew he was going to be all right – there would be no severe reprimand or worse. They discussed the match, Uzzell's part in it, the All Blacks and rugby in general before the student was allowed to return to his studies and life carried on.

Saturday would see the visit of Ebbw Vale to Rodney Parade and with Uzzell back at college and Glyn Davidge needing a deserved rest, the Newport selectors called up Eddie Mogford to play alongside Brian Jones in the centre and Bill Morris to take over at number eight. The Steelmen must have had high hopes of becoming the first team to defeat the first team to defeat the All Blacks, but they were unfounded. While Newport recorded a comfortable 12–0 victory, a much changed New Zealand XV was finding life difficult against the combined forces of Aberavon & Neath in Port Talbot. With five minutes remaining, the teams were tied at 6–6 before a late try from Ken Gray converted by Don Clarke got the tour back on track. A midweek visit to Abertillery Park to play Abertillery & Ebbw Vale was next on the itinerary, and among the 18,000 spectators at the fixture were Ray Cheney, Graham Bevan and Bob Prosser, keen to see how two of Monmouthshire's most famous clubs would rise to the challenge. The tourists ran out winners by 13 points to nil in what was the second of their nine matches to be played in November. The itinerary would take them to London, Cambridge and Scotland before returning to Wales for the eagerly anticipated encounter with Cardiff later in the month. Newport also had a busy agenda with six matches to play during the month. Clearly the club would be beaten at some stage in the coming weeks, but while Ebbw Vale had not proved equal to the task, next up were three away matches at Cardiff, Cambridge University and, rather soon after the home fixture, a trip up the valley to Ebbw Vale.

In 1892 the administrators who ran rugby union made the momentous decision to completely overhaul the method of scoring that had been in place since the game's inception. Where once the number of goals and tries scored would determine the outcome of a match, from the 1892–3 season these scores would be translated into points and, but for a few variations in the value of tries and drop goals, the system remains in place today. The record books confirm several instances when Newport RFC lost three games in succession, but never before had the club lost three consecutively without scoring any points. In the immediate aftermath of Newport's finest hour, came a run of three defeats at Cardiff, Cambridge University and Ebbw Vale that saw the hottest names in Welsh rugby fail to trouble the scoreboard. Great rivals Cardiff in particular would have revelled in the 3–0 victory that saw them become the first club to down the Black and Ambers following Newport's famous victory. That two players from the line-up were absent would not have mattered a jot, Eddie Mogford continuing in the centre and Barry Edwards included at full-back. Seven days later the students of Cambridge University recorded a convincing 14–0 victory, before the trip to Ebbw Vale compounded the misery, the visitors going down by six points to nil. At Eugene Cross Park, David Husband replaced Ian Ford in the second row with Mogford retained in the centre. Elsewhere this was the side that had played against New Zealand and, as at Cardiff, there would be no excuses made, no reason for the defeats other than meeting a better team on the day. Similarly, Newport had no complaints when losing to Cambridge University, but extenuating circumstances saw ten changes in personnel without which the club, if not winning the game, may well have registered some points to avoid the third whitewash.

The extenuating circumstances were brought about by the WRU's decision to hold trial matches earlier in the season than was normal practice, but essential with Wales due to play New Zealand in Cardiff on 21 December. For the first trial held at Rodney Parade on 16 November, the selectors invited Dick Uzzell, David Watkins, Brian Price, Brian Cresswell, Glyn Davidge and Algy Thomas to line-up for the Reds with Ray Cheney selected at full-back for the Whites. Cresswell's selection somewhat goes against the advances made in sports science over the past 50 years. Today, it would be unheard of for a player who had sustained such damage to the delicate tissues that are incorporated in and around the structure of the knee to resume playing in less than three weeks. Undoubtedly heavily strapped up and bandaged, not only did Brian Cresswell take his place in the Reds but he was also asked to captain the team. This was the player's last tilt at international honours, but it wasn't to be. Neither did Cresswell make another first-team appearance for Newport after playing against Wasps. It was Newport United that enjoyed his services before he accepted an invitation from Ron Jones to play a few end of season games at Abertillery where he formed an international back row alongside Haydn Morgan and Alun Pask.

With seven players on duty at the trial and Dennis Perrott also on standby as a reserve, it was a much under strength Newport that travelled to Grange Road. All those involved would have been well aware this was a ground at which the club had failed to record a victory since 1949. The six away matches against Cambridge University played in the intervening years had all ended in defeat, so maybe it shouldn't have come as any great surprise when yet another cross-country trek saw the team return empty handed.

The sports pages of the national newspapers that hit the stands on 31 October gave ample coverage to the previous day's upset at Rodney Parade, but elsewhere they may also have published the latest pop chart which showed that Brian Poole and the Tremeloes' stint at number one was over. Gerry and the Pacemakers were enjoying a third consecutive chart topping disc with 'You'll Never Walk Alone', a song that would be adopted by the Kop at Anfield, home of Liverpool Football Club. At number two was 'She Loves You', the Beatles' third single that spent four weeks at number one in September and would reclaim the coveted position at the end of November completing a total of 18 weeks in the top three.

In a few short months the record-buying public had helped launch several new groups into the spotlight, little realising the part they were playing in the changing face of music. The charts confirmed there was still an interest in the recordings of stars such as Jimmy Young, Karl Denver, Frank Ifield, and Ken Dodd while Cliff Richard and Elvis Presley would more than hold their own for some years to come. Instrumentals were still proving popular and room could always be found for a novelty item if it hit the spot. In November 1963 this arrived courtesy of Allan Sherman, an American comedian whose 'Hello Muddah Hello Fadduh!' told of a young lad who was pretty pissed off at being sent to summer camp where it did nothing but rain and was writing a missive to his parents begging to be allowed back home – that is until the sun broke through.

There would certainly have been large sections of the British public which remained oblivious to all that was happening in the world of popular music, but the night of 4 November changed that unsuspecting innocence forever. This was the occasion of the annual Royal Command Variety Performance which, in 1963, was held at the Prince of Wales Theatre in London's West End. Queen Elizabeth, the Queen Mother and Princess Margaret, together with her husband Lord Snowdon, were the royal guests and the line-up chosen for their entertainment was a stellar list of popular artists of the day including: Marlene Dietrich, Harry Secombe, Pinky and Perky, Eric Sykes and Sophie Tucker. Also invited to perform were the Beatles and, as the group prepared to sing 'Twist and Shout', their fourth and final number, the inimitable John Lennon acknowledged the division of wealth and social status reflected in the audience. "Will the people in the cheaper seats clap your hands? All the rest of you, if you'll just rattle your jewellery." Another defining moment in the bigger picture that the 1960s would come to represent.

Nobody could ever suggest the eastern valleys of south Wales was an area that spawned any divisions of class. This was a region built on strict work ethics, hard graft and manual labour and, as such, was populated in the main by the working classes. Nothing wrong with that, but in early November there were dastardly deeds being discussed behind closed doors and they reached way beyond any issues pertaining to class. They hit right at the very heart of society, at the wide gap that still existed between men and women. Bucking a long list of male officials, the urban district council of Pontypool had recently elected a lady mayor. Councillor Francis Maud Prosser was enjoying her term of office, enjoying representing the town at official functions and proving to be a worthy holder of a position that was highly respected. With the New Zealand All Blacks due to play a combined Pontypool & Cross Keys at Pontypool Park on Wednesday, 27 November, arrangements were in hand finalising the details of the VIPs who were to be invited to attend the match and official reception that would take place following the rugby. When the invitations were dispatched there was one glaring omission, Councillor Prosser was not on the guest list.

Looking at the crowd scenes included in the footage of the Newport/New Zealand match, there is a notable absence of female faces among the thousands of spectators on the terraces. Ladies were present, but they were more likely to be found in the relative comfort offered by the grandstand rather than exposed to the elements among the male dominated crowd of supporters looking on from the touchlines. There can be no getting away from the fact that 50 years ago rugby was a sport organised by men and played by men for the entertainment of men. Not surprising then, that when the committee members of the Pontypool and Cross Keys rugby clubs got together to arrange the guest lists they agreed, or maybe conspired, to exclude the mayor of the town in which the match was to be played. Councillor Trevor Vaughan had attended the Newport match and wherever the All Blacks played similar courtesies would be extended to such elected officials, but not in Pontypool – big mistake!

Pontypool Park was not only the home of Pontypool RFC but was a large area of grass verges and wooded fringes that was accessible to all. It was there for the people to enjoy and, most importantly, came under the auspices of the district council. It was not for the officials of the local rugby club to treat as their own and when the lady mayor was excluded from the plans, the message sent out was loud and clear – think again or find somewhere else to go and kick your ball about. With the match less than three weeks away, the matter needed resolving as soon as possible and it is no surprise to learn that the bigwigs at the respective clubs made a hasty U-turn, Councillor Prosser received her invitation and the issue was defused and quickly forgotten by all barring those red faces who would have to entertain the mayor on the day.

Events taking place a few miles up the road would not have escaped the attention of those at Newport RFC but truth be known, come the end of November it was how the All Blacks were performing on the field that was of interest, rather than any political shenanigans being played out behind closed doors. While Newport was struggling to get any points on the scoreboard, the tourists were making their way around Britain with reports suggesting they were improving with every match played. At Twickenham they ran in seven tries against the London Counties and four more against Cambridge University. Then it was north of the border, to Hawick where the South of Scotland put up a spirited display before going down 8–0. A combined Glasgow & Edinburgh had no answer to New Zealand up front, and eight more tries were scored in an impressive 33–3 victory, one without Don Clarke who was rested after playing in the first eight matches. Looking at the tour itinerary 50 years on, the first thing that stands out is how the All Blacks were moved around Britain with little consideration given to the travelling times involved. After playing two matches in Scotland in November, the tourists would return north in January when another two featured on the itinerary. Similarly, there would be two visits to Ireland. There may well have been good reasoning behind what appears to be a sequence of badly thought-out travel arrangements, but the next stage of the tour saw the party leave Glasgow and head south for a return visit to Wales. The All Blacks must have arrived back at the Seabank Hotel in Porthcawl before news broke of an incident some 4,000 miles away that sent shock waves around the world. A few hours' travelling, a game of rugby and pretty much everything else was put in perspective by events in Dallas, images of which were being transmitted and reported as the British public was about to sit down for Friday's evening meal.

It is probably the definitive 'Where were you when you heard the news?' moment. Where were you when you heard about the shooting of John Fitzgerald Kennedy, the 35th President of the United States of America? JFK was the youngest president elected to office when he gained a narrow majority over the Republican candidate Richard Nixon in the 1960 election. Kennedy was also the first Roman Catholic president and the first of purely Irish descent. This was recognised as recently as the summer of '63 when he visited Ireland as part of a tour of Europe best remembered for his 'Ich bin ein Berliner...' speech made in West Berlin on 26 June. It was a little over three years since the election held on the first Tuesday in November saw the Democrats win back the White House, and now a man many were predicting would become one of the great political figures of the 20th century was dead.

A red X marks the spot on Elm Street in downtown Dallas where Kennedy was struck by an assassin's bullet as his motorcade slowly made its way west along the thoroughfare. The shooting took place shortly after noon Central Standard Time on Friday, 22 November, six hours behind British Standard Time. The names of Lee Harvey Oswald and Jack Ruby would make the headlines in the following days, Harvey accused of the killing and Ruby his self-appointed executioner. Graphic photographs show the sequence of events as the motorcade passed in front of the Texas School Book Depository. It was from the sixth floor of the redbrick building that Oswald fired at least three shots taking down the president and critically injuring John Connally, Governor of Texas. Stills clearly showing Jackie Kennedy holding her husband in her arms make for sombre inspection but perhaps the most dramatic image of all is that of the moment two days later when nightclub owner, Jack Ruby, somehow managed to get to within point-blank range of Oswald as he was being led from the basement of police headquarters by officers escorting him to the county jail. Here we see Ruby pointing the .38 revolver, the look on Oswald's face as he recoils from the impact and the shocked reactions shown by those standing nearby. The incident was also shown live on American television to an audience that numbered several million.

In a year that can boast many highs and lows which have left an indelible mark on the historical landscape of Britain, it is the shooting of a political figure in the United States that made the biggest impact. The world's press and television networks had a story that would dominate the front pages and news reports for days and indeed, weeks. One is always left pondering what would have made those front pages and headlines had a story, such as the assassination of an American president, not broken. Somehow those reams and reams of newspaper would have been filled and the hours of television news programmes broadcast – something would have been deemed newsworthy enough to fill the void. If it had been released on any other Friday the Beatle's second long-playing record would have claimed more than a passing reference in the media. It was one of the group's finest albums but the acclaim it undoubtedly deserved would have to wait for another day.

As New Zealand rattled up the victories so did the Newport players, officials and supporters begin to consider the fanciful idea that it might just be possible that no other side would achieve what the club had and that New Zealand would return home with just the one defeat spoiling an otherwise perfect record. Dreaming maybe, but when Newport travelled to Old Deer Park to play London Welsh, more than a little interest was directed towards the Arms Park where the tourists were playing Cardiff. London Welsh faced a Newport team that included 13 members of the side that had played against the All Blacks, only changes in the middle of the field disrupting the winning combination. David Watkins was rested, and his place taken by Brian Jones moving from centre where Roddy Jones now partnered Eddie Mogford. A minute's silence was observed at Old Deer Park, a few brief moments for contemplation and reflection that was undoubtedly replicated at all sports venues throughout the country. The Black and Ambers returned to winning ways with a solid performance that resulted in a 19–12 victory. This was the start of a run of success that would extend to the turn of the year. Newport won the remaining seven matches played during the last week of November and through December.

What of New Zealand? How were the All Blacks faring against a side expected to make life difficult, a side that had tasted victory against the tourists ten years earlier? Several Newport players confess they were willing New Zealand to victory, hoping for a result that would not only see the club's great rivals put in their place, but one of the more demanding fixtures safely negotiated. News filtered through that Cardiff were winning 5–3 and should have been further ahead but for a series of missed kicks at goal. Everyone at Old Deer Park was cheering the Blue and Blacks on to victory except the Newport players and officials, together with any travelling supporters who were silently praying that the men in black would prevail. Everything was crossed. That the All Blacks won the match by the closest of margins, thanks to a drop goal by Mac Herewini, was welcome news in the Newport camp, but how would this attitude hold up when Wales played the tourists? Where would loyalties lie then? An exception could well be made but then again, maybe not.

There was no doubting where any loyalties lay when New Zealand played Pontypool & Cross Keys the following Wednesday. There was no love lost between the Valleys clubs and Newport, which was ever viewed with great suspicion as the steady stream of players from the smaller clubs gravitated south. It would not have gone unnoticed by supporters at Pontypool and Cross Keys that, included in the Newport team which defeated the All Blacks, were six players who had played club rugby either at Pontypool Park or across the valley at Pandy Park. Ray Cheney, Stuart Watkins, Dennis Perrott, David Watkins, Algy Thomas and Brian Price had all served part of their apprenticeships at one or other of the clubs, while David Jones and Dick Uzzell both flirted with opportunities to join the Keys.

When the All Blacks took the field at Pontypool Park, it is unlikely they paid any attention to someone who was sitting in one of the favoured seats in the middle of the grandstand. Councillor Francis Maud Prosser, Mayor of Pontypool took her rightful place among representatives of the two clubs and the New Zealand management. She would have been pleased with the performance of the combined team. Not expected to upset the tourists, the eight men from Cross Keys, together with seven players from Pontypool raised their game and the 18,000 spectators, most of whom were found on the enormous bank that overlooks the ground, had plenty to cheer. Admirably led by the incumbent Welsh captain, scrum-half Clive Rowlands, the combined team countered everything the All Blacks threw at them. It wasn't pretty and the outcome was never in any doubt but as the match entered its final minutes, the scoreboard showed the tourists leading 6–0. A late try by Ian Smith, converted by Clarke, took the score to 11–0 at the final whistle. Almost a third of the way into the tour, New Zealand fielded a side that had the look of a second XV about it. Only Don Clarke, three-quarter Malcolm Dick and scrum-half Kevin Briscoe would face Wales in a little under four weeks' time, but for Rowlands it was an early opportunity to play against the man likely to line-up against him in Cardiff and he would certainly have studied the New Zealand full-back's reaction to the various probing kicks the scrum-half launched in his direction. There would be plenty more heading Clarke's way at Cardiff Arms Park; the likely Welsh skipper on the day had started to do his homework.

With the first international a week away, the South-Western Counties had the misfortune to face an All Blacks team that had the appearance of a Test side. Twelve of the New Zealanders who played at Exeter would face Ireland in Dublin, and the home team had no answer to the All Black forward platform which laid the foundation for the highest score the tourists would register on the European sector of the tour. They ran in nine tries, seven by the backs, to run out eventual winners by 38 points to six and end November with eleven of the twelve matches played won, a much healthier position than a month earlier.

While New Zealand were running riot in Devon, Newport ended November with a comfortable 26–5 home win against Llanelli. In defeating London Welsh and now the Scarlets, the Black and Ambers had put the run of three defeats behind them. Six matches in December would see the year out, a year that hadn't seen any club rugby until March but which would still end with Newport playing 42 matches. For New

Zealand, December would include nine matches, among them internationals against Ireland and Wales. England would be the first game in the new year, with Scotland two weeks later. Among the other remaining fixtures perhaps it was Munster, the Western Counties and Llanelli who fancied their chances more than others. They could each look forward to playing the tourists either immediately before one of the internationals or a few days after, games in which some star players might be rested. Meanwhile, all they could do in Newport was watch on with interest, honorary New Zealanders in all but name excepting on Saturday, 21 December, when not only would Wales be looking to extend the winning sequence of victories against the All Blacks, but hopefully with a team that included a number of Newport players.

CHAPTER EIGHT

They'll Never Forget Newport

"Some people think football is a matter of life and death…
I can assure them it is much more serious than that."
Bill Shankly (1914–81)

As 1963 ENTERED its final month and with the countdown
to Christmas well under way, the archivists at the BBC set
about the task of compiling the best of the year's footage in
preparation for the annual BBC *Sports Personality of the Year*
awards' programme to be screened live from Broadcasting
House in front of an invited audience of Britain's finest
sportsmen and sportswomen.

The extreme weather had done its best to disrupt the
sporting calendar in the early months of the year and while
snow and ice certainly succeeded in causing chaos and misery,
this was only a temporary diversion – sport eventually winning
the day, even if the fixture lists did become a bit congested
as the various seasons drew to a close. The Five Nations
Championship got under way in January despite the odds
stacked against it running to schedule. After defeating Wales
in Cardiff, England marched on to the title, only a scoreless
draw with Ireland in Dublin preventing a Triple Crown and
Grand Slam. In the 13-man game Wakefield Trinity retained
the Challenge Cup, with Swinton and Hunslet sharing the
League Championship.

151

Association football's two major titles went to the northwest. Everton were crowned First Division Champions and it was Manchester United who won the FA Cup when defeating Leicester City 3–1 in the final at Wembley. North of the border Rangers completed a notable double winning the Scottish League and Scottish Cup. And in May it was Tottenham Hotspur that carried the flag into Europe, emphatic winners of the European Cup Winners' Cup when defeating Atlético Madrid 5–1 in the final held in Rotterdam.

In the early days of live outside broadcasts, the Boat Race was one of the biggest sporting events covered by the BBC, the cameras and commentators having to follow the crews as they travelled the four and a quarter miles of the Thames that stretch from Putney to Mortlake. Camera crews would be positioned along the river banks and aboard various craft on the water to record the race as it unfolded. In 1963 it was the dark blues of Oxford University that reached the finish line first, but the betting odds on what is effectively a two-horse race would not have been attractive to punters, unlike those on offer at the most viewed sporting event of the year which took place at Aintree racecourse on the outskirts of Liverpool.

Black and white footage of the Grand National confirms the progress made by animal rights campaigners and the RSPCA in their ongoing efforts to make the world's most famous steeplechase a safer journey for horse and rider. The fences now are noticeably smaller, the number of runners has been reduced to a maximum of 40 and the cavalry charge to the first obstacle somewhat contained, but in 1963 it was more akin to the Charge of the Light Brigade as the runners and riders set off on the four and a half mile journey that would see one of them enter horse racing's hall of fame.

The name Piggott is most associated with flat racing, but it was Lester's father Keith who had his name added to the list of Grand National winners and their connections when he trained a horse he also co-owned with the celebrated coiffeur 'Teasy Weasy' Raymond. The bookies obviously didn't rate the horse's chances very highly when sending Ayala ridden by Pat Buckley off at odds of 66/1, but the Grand National is a race with a history of upsets and 1963 witnessed one of the biggest giving the on-course bookies and betting shops across the nation a big payday, a relatively small percentage of the millions of pounds gambled on the race returned on winning bets. Two months later the odds were a generous 5/1 for a Derby favourite, but punters took advantage of them and were rewarded when the French trained Relko ridden by Yves Saint-Martin stormed up the Epsom straight to win the Blue Riband of British flat racing.

The sound of leather being struck by willow echoed around the county grounds as the West Indies' cricketers, under the captaincy of Frank Worrell, tore into England, winning the Test series 3–1. Fast bowlers Charlie Griffith and Wes Hall caused much of the damage with the ball, and the batsmen led by Garfield Sobers notched up the runs. Great stuff, and all those kids who once would have wanted to be England when settling down to a game of 'Howzat!' were now shifting their allegiances, each knowing the West Indies' line-up by heart.

Earlier in the year England's cricketers had toured Australia. Against Victoria, Colin Cowdrey scored an impressive 307 runs, which prompted an unexpected reaction from a vehicle licensing department in Caernarvon of all places. For reasons best known to their owners alone, personalised number plates have become something of a status symbol, but in 1963 they were rarely spotted. Colin Cowdrey, or to give him his full name, Michael Colin Cowdrey, would have been surprised to receive a communication from the Welsh council offering him the registration number MCC 307. The paperwork could be easily arranged – did the English cricketer want it? Yes was the answer, and Colin Cowdrey became the owner of car registration number MCC 307 which had the double connotation of the abbreviated Marylebone Cricket Club – he couldn't say no!

Team sports and partnerships with horses aside, the individual performers who made the headlines during the year were a mix of home-grown talent and those from overseas. The Championships at Wimbledon saw the American Chuck McKinley win what would be his only singles Grand Slam title. He beat Australian Fred Stolle in the final 9–7, 6–1, 6–4 and had the distinction of not dropping a set throughout the tournament. The Australian queen of the court, Margaret Smith, won the ladies' singles title, while in golf New Zealander Bob Charles proved there were other sports played in his country when winning the Open Championship at Royal Lytham & St Annes. In a 36-hole play-off, Charles beat the American Phil Rodgers by seven shots to win his only major and the £1,500 prize money.

Home success in individual international competition came when Scotland's Jim Clarke won the Formula One Championship driving a Lotus Climax, but the biggest story of the year featuring a British sportsman unfolded at Wembley Arena on the night of 18 June. In a non-title fight, boxer Henry Cooper faced the Olympic heavyweight champion from the Rome games of 1960, the then-named Cassius Clay, the first of two contests between the fighters, but the more memorable. Clay insisted he was distracted by Elizabeth Taylor sitting ringside with her husband Richard Burton when he felt the full weight of "enry's 'ammer' crash into his jaw, and the next thing he knew he was on the floor with the referee standing over him and counting. The clock was ticking down the seconds at the end of the third round and the count had only reached four when the bell went and Clay staggered back to his corner clearly the worse for wear. The story of the torn glove and the time trainer Angelo Dundee engineered which allowed Clay a few extra moments on the stool as a replacement was put on, leaves most questions unanswered but the distraction was sufficient to clear the head and the American began the fourth round desperate to get the job done. A cut eye brought Cooper's fight to an end, but he could hold his head high – he had floored a man destined to become the greatest heavyweight boxer of them all.

Somewhere in the bowels of the BBC Television Centre footage of all these great sporting occasions was being edited for the clips that would cover each sport on the night. Where would the winner come from? Before the evening could reach its climax there were other awards to be presented. Firstly, that for the best team performance of the year was given to the West Indies cricketers – clearly the adjudicators had not been at Rodney Parade in October. Then it was the turn of the overseas personality which went to the French cyclist Jacques Anquetil who had completed a hat-trick of consecutive victories in the prestigious Tour de France. Then it was time for the main presentation of the evening In third place was Jim Clarke and it was another Scot, swimmer Bobby McGregor, who was the runner-up but who was about to be crowned BBC Sports Personality of the Year for 1963?

Twelve months earlier the podium had been the domain of sportswomen. The swimmers Anita Lonsborough and Linda Ludgrove were joined by track star Dorothy Hyman, Ludgrove in third place, Hyman second and Lonsborough that year's winner. Hyman had enjoyed an outstanding twelve months, winning gold in the 100m at the European Championships held in Belgrade, together with silver in the 200m and bronze in the 4 x 100m relay. The Commonwealth Games had taken place in Perth, Australia in 1962 where Dorothy Hyman had won gold in the 100yds and 220yds and silver in the 4 x 110yds relay. This period of success may well have been the peak of a fine career but twelve months later it was the sprinter who the BBC crowned as its sports personality of 1963.

Not to be outdone by events in London, BBC Wales had launched a Welsh equivalent in 1954, when the first recipient was rugby and athletics star, Ken Jones. The Newport wing three-quarter was joined on the honours list by hooker Bryn Meredith in 1962, but in 1963 it was the turn of boxing. In July British Flyweight Champion Howard Winstone fought Alberto Serti for his European crown, knocking the Italian out in the 14th round. Winstone immediately put both British and European titles on the line when he fought Billy Calvert, winning the contest on points. In December he was back in the ring, this time against John O'Brien and again both titles were up for grabs. Another points' decision went the way of the little Welshman from Merthyr and nobody could deny him the title of BBC Wales Sports Personality of the Year for 1963.

Following the big win against the South-Western Counties, the All Blacks confirmed they were well and truly running into form with another resounding victory against the Midland Counties in a match played at Coundon Road, Coventry on 3 December. This fixture presents us with something of a conundrum. Who were the tourists scheduled to play at Welford Road, Leicester on 28 December? – the Midland Counties. Surely the same team could have two shots at the tourists? Well, yes and no. Close inspection confirms that in the first of the matches, New Zealand would face a team largely made up of players from the Coventry and Moseley clubs, and in the second it would be players from Bedford, Leicester and Northampton that would dominate selection. All a bit confusing but it meant nothing to the All Blacks who cut loose at Coventry against a side from which much was expected. Seven tries were scored to add to the eight registered four days earlier, the tourists comfortably winning the match by 37 points to nine. That seven of the team would play against Ireland on Saturday confirms these All Blacks were in no way inhibited by the prospect of injuries to leading players. They were on a mission to win all the remaining matches and if there were casualties to accommodate, then so be it.

With major tours a thing of the past these days, if supporters want to see the southern hemisphere teams play, with very rare exceptions this inevitably means a trip to either Twickenham, Murrayfield, the Millennium Stadium or the Aviva Stadium. Wilson Whineray's fifth All Blacks played at the Aviva Stadium, although it wasn't known as such in 1963. Back then it was called Lansdowne Road, a name that still resonates with most Irish supporters no matter what the sign above the gate may read. After racking up 75 points in their previous two matches, the All Blacks were a confident team going into the first of the five Tests. That Ireland had failed to beat New Zealand in their four previous meetings was an irrelevance, but with the benefit of hindsight and the knowledge that 50 years and 22 matches later, the men in green have yet to defeat the All Blacks, Lansdowne Road, Dublin on 7 December 1963 was as good an opportunity as they have ever had. The home side were leading 5–0 approaching half-time, but a try by Kel Tremain reduced the deficit at the interval. How many times the boot of Don Clarke rescued the All Blacks during his international career is a matter for debate, but once again a penalty goal took the visitors into a 6–5 lead that they held until the final whistle.

As Ireland and New Zealand battled it out in Dublin, the Welsh selectors were in attendance at the final trial match which showcased the players in contention for selection against the tourists in two weeks. Brian Price, Algy Thomas, David Watkins, Dick Uzzell and Ray Cheney were Newport's representatives in Cardiff, which meant it was all change at Rodney Parade where Bristol were the visitors. David Husband was called up to join Ian Ford in the second row, Richard Smith replaced Thomas on the open-side and it was a re-jigged midfield where Brian Jones took over at outside-half and a new centre pairing was introduced. Eddy Mogford had stepped up on previous occasions when Uzzell was unavailable, but for Dennis Perrott this was a new experience. Happy on either wing, Perrott now found himself closer to the action but, given a half chance he would exploit the confines of the midfield – there is no substitute for pace and Perrott had that in abundance. John Hughes stood in for Cheney at full-back and Newport set about avenging the early season defeat at the Memorial Ground. That 0–16 reverse would be the heaviest loss suffered by the club in 1963, and credit should be given to a team that may have included a new look back division but ran out 9–3 winners.

The Combined Services visited Rodney Parade on Monday and later in the week the club had a difficult away match at Aberavon. Price, Thomas and Cheney returned against the Services with Jones, Mogford and Perrott continuing in midfield. Against Aberavon, Price took his place in the second row, Thomas stood down and still there was no David Watkins or Dick Uzzell on the team sheet. Newport continued its winning streak but there was much more to celebrate at the club when news broke of the Welsh team selected to play New Zealand. Brian Price and David Watkins were surely among the first names pencilled in, but when Algy Thomas and John Uzzell were selected to win first caps, it rubber-stamped Newport's great victory.

Comparatively few players get selected to play for Wales. Some aren't good enough, while others have to accept there are better players around who will always gain preference. The Newport players who plotted New Zealand's downfall experienced mixed fortunes when it came to international rugby. Ray Cheney never played for his country, ever the bridesmaid never the bride. Stuart Watkins would win his first cap against Scotland in the new year, while Dennis Perrott still ponders over what might have been if Uzzell had moved the ball to the left instead of drop kicking his name into the record books. Brian Jones, Ian Ford and Glyn Davidge each played for Wales with distinction, but their day had passed. The front-row men were no lesser players for missing out on the bigger stage, which leaves Bob Prosser and Keith Poole. Prosser played in the same position as the then current Welsh captain, Clive Rowlands, which automatically limited his chance of international honours in the short term. As for Keith Poole? Still new to senior rugby, Poole was not going to get the call up, nobody expected him to, least of all the player himself, but as the years passed and he put in outstanding performances match after match, season after season, his chance must surely come – Keith Poole would one day play for Wales, but he didn't.

Poole could only watch on as Bridgend's Gary Prothero

enjoyed an extended run in the Welsh team. When that player's career was cut short due to a serious eye injury, the selectors turned to Newbridge's Ken Braddock, then Ron Jones who was playing his rugby at Coventry, before reappraising the talent to be found in Monmouthshire. Once more it was the Newbridge club that celebrated when Dennis Hughes was called up for international duty before Neath's Dai Morris would make the position his own. For many followers of the game in Wales, his team mates not least among them, Keith Poole remains the most outstanding rugby player of his generation not to be capped by his country.

Algy Thomas and Dick Uzzell were the only new caps in the Welsh team, the selectors opting for experienced players, men proven in their individual positions. Grahame Hodgson continued at full-back, with Robert Morgan and Dewi Bebb on the wings. Oxford University student Ken Jones, who had played against the All Blacks in the opening match of the tour, was Uzzell's centre partner with Clive Rowlands and David Watkins at half-back. The combination of Denzil Williams, Norman Gale and Len Cunningham made a solid front row, Brian Price and Brian Thomas would be more than comfortable against whatever pairing New Zealand decided to pitch against them. Dai Hayward, Alun Pask and Thomas were a fast trio of loose forwards, each comfortable ball in hand. Only Llanelli's Robert Morgan and Norman Gale had yet to play against the tourists, while in Clive Rowlands, Dewi Bebb, Brian Price and Dai Hayward, Wales had the benefit of four men who had captained teams against New Zealand earlier in the tour.

With Ireland beaten, New Zealand could now focus attention on the Wales match. Of the 36 fixtures on the itinerary, this was the one that stood out above all others – Wales had to be beaten. The ghosts of 1905 still reared their head whenever the two countries met, and New Zealand were yet to defeat Wales at Cardiff Arms Park, the 1924 match played at Swansea. There would be much at stake come 21 December but with three fixtures to fulfil first, the tourists had plenty to occupy them. Following the international in Dublin, the All Blacks headed west to Limerick to play Munster, a match that locals predicted would result in a famous win for the home team. That New Zealand could make 13 changes for the match, one of them positional, and defeat a strong Munster in front of an enthusiastic home crowd, shows how well the squad had adapted to the demands of a lengthy tour. Munster didn't disappoint, taking the game to the All Blacks at every opportunity but it wasn't to be. Few would have denied the home team a draw but New Zealand showed great resolve to hang on for a 6–3 victory.

The party returned to Wales for another extended stay at their Porthcawl base from where they would travel to Swansea and Bristol for their next two games and remain in residence for the build-up to the Wales match. Don Clarke was struggling with a groin injury which prevented him playing in Limerick, and he would not be included against Swansea or the Western Counties. Following the try fest that had seen the All Blacks cross for 15 in the two matches played before they departed for Ireland, they had only scored one in Dublin and one in Limerick. This downturn was soon reversed, but how the old scoring system so often failed to give a real indication of the balance of play is confirmed by the result at St Helen's. New Zealand beat Swansea 16–9 but, in doing so, scored four tries while the home team's points came courtesy of two penalties and a drop goal. Four more tries were scored in Bristol on Tuesday when the tourists defeated the cream of Gloucestershire and Somerset, 22–14.

A gap in the fixture list saw Newport inactive after the visit to Aberavon. The club would not play again before Christmas but, with four players in the Welsh team, there was much to look forward to and Newport's allocation of international tickets was quickly snapped up by members keen to see how Wales would fare against the tourists. Brian Price and David

Watkins had played during a disappointing Five Nations Championship earlier in the year that saw Wales win just one match when beating Scotland at Murrayfield. This was a torrid affair, best remembered for the 111 line-outs contested during the 80 minutes, a figure that takes some believing even with the benefit of television footage and documentary evidence. Welsh supporters needed something to remember the year by and beating New Zealand would provide the fillip their oft-tested patience deserved. There was a late change to the Welsh team when Ebbw Vale prop Denzil Williams was forced to withdraw, his place taken by Kingsley Jones of Cardiff, a seasoned international who had toured South Africa with the British Lions in 1962.

The opening exchanges confirmed that, come the final whistle, Newport would remain the only blemish on a record that was looking more impressive as the weeks unfolded. The Welsh pack were swept aside by an All Black eight that produced its finest performance of the tour to date. Returned to the team, Don Clarke peppered the Welsh posts with some long-distance efforts before converting an easy goal from 15 yards out. Few opportunities came the way of the Welsh backs in a match dominated by the visitors' forwards. Dick Uzzell did create a half chance when he wrong-footed the New Zealand defence and cut in towards the posts, only to see his pass to Brian Price go to ground five yards out with the line apparently at the second row's mercy. Such things happen, but even a converted try would not have been enough to claim the spoils, a second-half drop goal seeing the All Blacks home by six points to nil. The match ended on an unsavoury note when Welsh captain Clive Rowlands was unceremoniously charged in the back by Colin Meads as he made a mark inside the Welsh 25-yard line. The crowd was incensed and let its feelings known as the scrum-half was carried from the field on a stretcher after suffering a few frightening moments during which he lost all feeling. Lucky seems an inappropriate word, but what proved to be a jarred disc could have been so much worse. Rowlands would lead Wales out at Twickenham in the new year, but such injuries were a reminder of the risks involved when playing the most physical of sports.

Mementoes of the big occasions are usually limited to the match day programme, maybe a ticket or a menu from the official dinner and newspaper cuttings of the various press reports. For the players there is one other item that often finds its way into the kitbag – your opponent's jersey. A New Zealand jersey, the black one with the silver fern, now that would be something to show the grandchildren. Algy Thomas and Dick Uzzell would have been delighted to have acquired such a rare treasure, but at what cost? In the heat of the moment the pair readily exchanged their red Welsh jerseys for a black one, but what if they never played for Wales again? Surely the jersey they wore when winning their first cap should be valued above all else?

Dick Uzzell remembers lying in bed at his parents' home in Deri on the Sunday morning when the indefatigable Algy Thomas came knocking. Realising what the pair had done, Algy was intent on retrieving the situation and plans were already in place that would see the accommodating Bryn Meredith give him a Welsh jersey from his collection. Brian Price would do the same for his cousin and the next stage of the scheme would involve the pair heading off to Porthcawl on a begging mission – could they keep the jerseys received, have theirs back and replace them with the substitutes? Simple really, but totally dependant on the goodwill of Derek Arnold and Waka Nathan.

The Seabank Hotel in Porthcawl overlooks the Bristol Channel, a fine spot to take in the sea air, blow the cobwebs away. Just how much the victory over Wales meant to the New Zealanders became apparent when the Newport players arrived at the hotel. The All Blacks were partying in the large lounge the hotel management had allocated them during their stay. The message was delivered confirming that two Welsh players were in reception and would like a word. Send them up came the reply, but before Algy Thomas and Dick Uzzell could join the party they had to pass the All Blacks' initiation test. The pair had to down in one a pint consisting of half Guinness and half milk. Unappealing at the best of times but, after the previous night's revelries, a tough ask. Thomas and Uzzell became honorary members of the All Blacks' inner circle and found their opposite numbers more than willing to make the exchange – this was, after all, the season of goodwill.

Twelve months earlier Rodney Parade was covered with straw as measures were put in place to ensure the holiday fixtures could be played. There was to be no repeat in 1963 as the club prepared for three matches on consecutive days, starting with the visit of the Watsonians on Boxing Day, followed by the UAU on Friday and an away match at Cross Keys on Saturday which would bring the curtain down on the first half of the season. All three games were won extending the run of success to eight, while New Zealand continued in similar vein defeating the Combined Services at Twickenham on Boxing Day before travelling to Leicester for the second meeting with the Midland Counties who were duly beaten for the second time. Bizarrely, the tourists then headed all the way back to west Wales to play Llanelli on New Year's Eve, before returning to London on what appears to have been an ongoing circumnavigation of the southern half of mainland Britain to prepare to meet England four days later. Llanelli upheld the reputation of Welsh clubs by giving the All Blacks another searching examination, taking an eight-point lead and reaching half-time 8–3 to the good. It wasn't to be. The All Blacks ran in four second-half tries to run out comfortable winners by 22 points to eight, but it had been a good day at the office for the Scarlets. A noble effort maybe, but certainly not good enough to claim victory against the New Zealand All Blacks – such heroics would have to wait for another day.

Fortunately for the tourists and the thousands of supporters looking forward to seeing them play in the new year, there would be no repeat of the severe weather experienced twelve months earlier. Twenty-one matches into the tour, the All Blacks would now play a further eight in Britain and Ireland before crossing the English Channel to France where four were scheduled including an international in Paris. Then it was back to Cardiff for the traditional end of tour finale against the Barbarians, following which they would head home via Canada, stopping in Vancouver for two games that would finally bring the curtain down on the great adventure. In other words, there was still a long way to go.

England had visited New Zealand in the summer and come away disappointed not to have salvaged at least a draw from the second Test. Now was their chance to redress the issue, the reigning European champions expected to mount a serious challenge to New Zealand's hopes of a Grand Slam. With no apologies offered, it wasn't just Newport followers who were willing the All Blacks to victory at Twickenham. All Welsh supporters readily boast that they support Wales first and whoever is playing England second, and they could raise a glass to New Zealand after the tourists' emphatic 14–0 victory. This was the same team that had beaten Wales barring the late withdrawal of Waka Nathan who had broken his jaw at Llanelli, his place in the back row going to new cap Brian Lochore, heralding the start of another international career that would impact around the rugby-playing world. England were beaten by a team that observers felt were doing little more than going through the motions, happy to run up another victory with comparative ease. Invincible they would not be, but there was still much to play for as the party left London for the north of England.

Rugby union was once an amateur sport. Quite simply, a player's amateur status was dependant on his receiving no payment for playing the game, a dictum that reached beyond any financial reward. If a club wanted to recognise an outstanding achievement by an individual player or team, then protocol determined a request be made to the WRU where it would receive the necessary consideration at the appropriate committee meeting. A player's amateur status could be jeopardised by the most innocuous of circumstances but such apparent bureaucracy and red tape was essential.

The Newport players may well have found it difficult to buy a drink in any public house in the town in the aftermath of their victory. Such generosity was only to be expected and could never be seen as anything but a goodwill gesture but, any material recognition, anything by way of a gift that had a monetary value was taboo unless it fell within certain parameters rigidly observed by the Union. The Newport committee wanted to have a blazer badge crafted to identify the wearer as a member of the team that beat New Zealand. That was fine, but the players would have to bear the cost of the garment and they each ended up paying £20 for a Daks blazer which would be worn with pride for years to come.

John Leleu was a wing forward who won four Welsh caps between 1959–60 and was currently with Llanelli and played against Whineray's All Blacks. Leleu was a representative for Ronson, the leading manufacturer of cigarette lighters. Newport's victory presented a golden opportunity for a public relations exercise, and it was Leleu who set the ball rolling, the end result of which seeing the Newport players, touch judge, committee members and Gwynn Walters, the match referee, all receiving a lighter suitably inscribed as a lasting memento of the day. Which leaves one wondering why players who were not allowed to receive any monetary reward for playing the game could happily smoke themselves into an early grave with the full blessing of the WRU.

The blazer badge and cigarette lighter were both given the green light but the Union's approval was not required when Lord Brecon, then Secretary of State for Wales and president of Newport Athletic Club, invited the team and officials to a dinner held at the Angel Hotel in Abergavenny on Tuesday,

21 January. Truth be told, few of the players remember much about the night other than that it started quietly with a few drinks which undoubtedly included a sherry or two, proceeded over dinner with wine and much else and ended with a whole lot more. It was a liquid evening that Brian Price can cast no light on whatsoever, the Newport captain only able to confirm that he had to be assisted to his bed by two abstainers – backs probably! He was unable to get to school the following day and remained very much under the weather before receiving a most unwelcome telephone call from Nick Carter in the late afternoon.

Newport were playing the Royal Navy that night and Price had not been selected to play after representing Wales against England at Twickenham the previous Saturday. His place would be filled by Bill Morris, but Carter had a mini crisis on his hands and the club captain was going to have to turn out – Morris was now needed in the back row. Price's first question was the obvious one – where was Davidge? Which in turn got the obvious reply – he's still unconscious. A good night was had by all then and it is gratifying to note that Newport defeated the Royal Navy 33–3, the highest number of points scored during the season. Davidge would have been proud, his long-standing belief that a tipple before a match being a good thing finally vindicated.

The White City Stadium in Manchester, Harrogate Show Ground, and Linksfield, Aberdeen are not among the more obvious rugby grounds in Britain, but it was at these venues that the All Blacks played the next three matches. The North-Western Counties, the North-Eastern Counties and the North of Scotland were all defeated, but it was at Harrogate that the tourists had to dig deep to avoid what would have been a most unexpected defeat. Under the captaincy of Mike Weston, who led England in New Zealand, the North-Eastern Counties raced into an eleven-point lead in as many minutes. Perhaps there were the first signs of fatigue among the All Blacks, eleven of the team having played at Twickenham a week earlier, but if that was the case then they were dispelled in the second half when the tourists somehow found the reserves, dug deep and ground out another victory.

Grand Slams do not come easily. They were up for grabs each year as the home nations and France contested the championship, but the record books confirm how difficult it was for one country to defeat the other four in the same campaign. Touring teams could win their own Grand Slam by doing the obvious and with Ireland, Wales and England already beaten, next up it was the turn of Scotland to try and stop the All Blacks. Don Clarke may well have been the finest goal kicker of his time, but against Scotland at Murrayfield and in front of the biggest crowd of the tour which was estimated at 80,000, he was way off the mark. Several long-range penalty attempts and drop goals were sent in the direction of the posts, but all failed to bisect the uprights and, for only the second time on tour, New Zealand were unable to register victory, more than contained by a Scottish team who might well have taken more from the game. They are virtually unknown in the 21st century but scoreless draws were not that uncommon 50 years ago and that was exactly how the match ended. There would be no Grand Slam for the tourists, while Scotland is still waiting for a first victory over the All Blacks, making that 0–0 draw a significant result for both countries. And down in Newport there was a huge sigh of relief – rugby immortality had just got that little bit nearer.

Twenty-six matches played – ten more and the tourists could start thinking about the journey home. Recent performances suggested they already were, but the return to Ireland to play Leinster in Dublin and Ulster in Belfast was enough to refocus the mind. The All Blacks would not have needed to read the back pages to know they were under-performing. The end of the tour may well have been in sight but it was far from over with at least five of the upcoming opponents considered to have every chance of victory. As is so often the case, it would be two of those teams given little or no chance that would go close to recording what would have been a major upset but neither was an Irish province. New Zealand left the Emerald Isle with two more notches on the belt. Leinster were beaten 11–8 and Ulster 24–5, a big disappointment following the 5–5 draw against Bob Stuart's fourth All Blacks ten years earlier.

The supporters who turned up at Rodney Parade to watch Newport play the Royal Navy on Wednesday night would have learnt of Leinster's defeat earlier in the day, and news of another victory in Ireland would have been confirmed at Stradey Park where the Black and Ambers were the visitors on Saturday. How far from Newport interest in the fortunes of the All Blacks extended is not known, but it is difficult to imagine those at clubs such as Llanelli not to have been closely following the final weeks of the tour. Who rugby supporters in Wales were hoping would prevail each time New Zealand took the field is a matter for conjecture, so intense was the inter-club rivalry on which the great achievements of the national team was once based. It would be reassuring to believe they were all firmly in Newport's corner, but one suspects otherwise. Not that it mattered. Newport RFC was slowly but surely nearing the end of what had become an emotional roller coaster in the three months since that famous afternoon at Rodney Parade.

The worst performance of the tour? That was probably against the South-Eastern Counties at Bournemouth on a day when Don Clarke missed eight of his nine kicks at goal. Both teams scored two tries, with Clarke's one success the difference between them at the final whistle. In a little over two weeks, New Zealand would return to Wales to bring the curtain down on the European sector of the tour with a match against the Barbarians, but now it was across the English Channel to France for four matches, with hopefully time found for some much needed R&R. Toulouse, Bordeaux, Paris, Lyon: four great cities in which to relax, enjoy the local produce, get some winter sun on the back and up the ante on the rugby field. The

All Blacks did all of that and much more while not losing sight of the main reason they were able to enjoy such delightful cities. When France B, South-West France, France and South-Eastern France were all defeated without too much inconvenience, the tourists could now focus on the party that had been arranged for them when the itinerary was put together twelve months earlier.

The Barbarians RFC is an institution within the rugby world. A club that doesn't have a home but one which every player would like to represent. The Barbarians only play a handful of fixtures during the season, most of which go back many years, but since 1947 the club had been invited to bring down the curtain on tours to Britain by Australia, South Africa and New Zealand. In 1962 the Barbarians were the only team to beat the fourth Springboks, so much was expected of them two years on. Newport's Brian Price and Stuart Watkins were included in a team that would be led by Ireland's Ronnie Dawson. Also invited to play was Ian Clarke, the All Black more than happy to line-up against men he had spent the past four months playing alongside. New Zealand had not asked for Gwynne Walters to referee any of the internationals, but the man who had officiated at Rodney Parade was appointed to take charge of the tour finale.

It may well have been the Mediterranean sun, those strolls along the boulevards of Paris, or simply the knowledge that they were on their way home. Whatever it was, the New Zealand players ran on to Cardiff Arms Park with a definite spring in the step. The All Blacks opened the scoring – that is to say Ian Clarke did. The prop called a mark some 35 yards out, and showed some of the skill that had apparently deserted his brother in recent weeks when dropping a sweet goal to put the Barbarians 3–0 ahead. From then on it was one-way traffic. Two unconverted tries by Kel Tremain and Colin Meads saw the tourists lead 6–3 at half time, but gave no indication of how the next 40 minutes would unfold. New Zealand played the best rugby of the tour, scoring six further tries all converted by

Don Clarke to run up 30 unanswered points. The biggest cheer was reserved for the last try of the match scored by Wilson Whineray after he threw an audacious dummy on his way to touching down under the posts leading to a rendition of 'For he's a jolly good fellow' from the crowd who appreciated they had witnessed a memorable moment. It was time to party.

The final log read played 34, won 32, drew one, lost one. A British Columbia Under 25 XV would lose a surprisingly close match 6–3 before New Zealand defeated British Columbia 39–3 giving extended statistics of played 36, won 34, drew one, lost one; the final record of Wilson Whineray's fifth New Zealand All Blacks who toured Europe and Canada in 1963–4.

One match lost. One blot on an otherwise damn near perfect record. Statistics may not always tell the truth, but they never lie. That Newport RFC was the only team to defeat a mighty New Zealand touring side is an achievement which cannot and should not be diminished. This was a memorable result not only for the club itself but for Welsh rugby in general, and it is a result that should be celebrated at every opportunity. There was a 25th-anniversary bash and another to mark the passing of 40 years since the famous day. Undoubtedly the surviving members of the Newport team will gather again to celebrate the 50th anniversary, remember the day Dick Uzzell's drop goal won a thrilling encounter against a star-studded New Zealand. Remember the day Wilson Whineray, Colin Meads, Brian Lochore, Waka Nathan, Kel Tremain, the Clarke brothers et al. ran out at Rodney Parade and remember the players who followed them. Fifteen players who would never take to the field in harness again, but on the day achieved fame and glory. Yes, at the end of the All Blacks' trek through Europe and Canada, so came the time to bestow rugby immortality on Ray Cheney, Stuart Watkins, Dick Uzzell, Brian Jones, Dennis Perrott, David Watkins, Bob Prosser, Neville Johnson, Graham

Bevan, David Jones, Ian Ford, Brian Price, Algy Thomas, Glyn Davidge and Keith Poole.

These players were not raising the roof at Cardiff Arms Park as Wales stormed to a Grand Slam-winning triumph, neither did they record great deeds with the British Lions in foreign climes. They were playing for their club, pulling on the jersey they wore week-in week-out. They were playing for Newport RFC, one of the most famous clubs in the world and on 30 October 1963 they delivered a result that stands at the top of a long list of famous victories recorded by the Black and Ambers. And it will continue to do so for as long as rugby football is played at Rodney Parade. As the *Western Mail* so perfectly put it – 'Now Is Their Hour' – and it always will be.

Afterword

"But be not afraid of greatness:
some men are born great, some achieve greatness,
and some have greatness thrust upon them."
William Shakespeare (1564–1616), *Twelfth Night* (1601)

WITH RUGBY UNION now a professional sport, the days of four- or five-month-long tours have disappeared. Such extended undertakings had, in fact, been completely overhauled before the advent of professionalism, with visiting teams playing far fewer matches than their predecessors were once accustomed to. The last extended tour undertaken by New Zealand was in 1972–3 when 32 matches were played, but subsequent visits saw the number considerably reduced: 18 in 1978; eleven in 1979; eight in 1983; and 13 in 1993. These figures not only confirm that fewer matches were played but that while the tours were shorter in duration they were also more frequent.

Since the arrival of the new millennium, rarely does a year pass when at least two and, on occasion, all three of the major rugby-playing southern hemisphere countries visit Europe. These tours take place in the autumn months and rarely are more than four matches played, all of which are against the home nations, France or Italy, with a midweek game rarely accommodated in the itinerary. The inevitable consequence of such short visits means that the days of a club playing in front of a full house against Australia, New Zealand or South Africa are over. From a Welsh perspective this is no bad thing, with club rugby now playing second fiddle to a structure that sees four regions playing at the highest level while the clubs compete in a league where, despite the high-scoring games that are regularly seen, the overall standard is not particularly good which, in turn, is reflected by the woeful attendances. Twenty-five thousand crammed into Rodney Parade to see Newport play? Dream on!

Victories against touring sides beyond the international arena were always rare occurrences. New Zealand had lost only three such matches before going down to Newport in 1963: at Swansea in 1935; against Cardiff in 1953; and South-West France had its day in Bordeaux in 1954. Slim pickings and much to be celebrated by the winning teams. Following on from Newport, it was nine years and one day before New Zealand suffered its next defeat in Britain, this against Llanelli at Stradey Park on 31 October 1972. A wonderful day saw the Scarlets beat the All Blacks 9–3, a magnificent victory that was rightly recognised throughout the rugby-playing world. Llanelli had joined Swansea, Cardiff and Newport on a very short roll of honour and Wales celebrated accordingly. Endlessly is perhaps a more apt word because to this very day if you didn't know any better, one could be forgiven for thinking that the only Welsh club to defeat a New Zealand touring team was Llanelli. Yes, the Scarlets' victory remains the most recent and for the reasons outlined above is almost certain to be the last, but exactly why is it remembered so favourably?

The 1971 British Lions had helped raise the profile of rugby union at home after winning the Test series on their tour of New Zealand. This was something no other Lions team had achieved before, or indeed since, and when the All Blacks arrived in Britain the following year, there was an early opportunity to restore some pride. It would prove to be the last big tour, the last time clubs, provinces and combined sides would get a crack at the mighty All Blacks. Thirty-two matches made up a demanding itinerary that included five internationals, a finale against the Barbarians and much else. Would this latest group of players to wear the silver fern be equal to the task?

The short answer is no. Again one is drawn to the statistics, and make of them what you will, but they confirm that of the 32 matches played, five were lost with two drawn – the worst record of any All Blacks side to visit Europe. If one considers the British sector of the tour in isolation, then the figures show that four of the 26 matches were lost with two drawn. Llanelli, North-Western Counties, Midland Counties West (the renamed Midland Counties East would also play the tourists) and the Barbarians defeated New Zealand, while Munster and Ireland claimed the two draws. Across the English Channel, France added to the misery when winning the final match of the tour in Paris.

Clearly Ian Kirkpatrick's All Blacks fell short of all that had gone before. One defeat in 1905–06, an invincible tour in 1924–5, three losses in 1935–6 followed by four in 1953–4 (two in France) and one in 1963–4 all provide better reading. There was also a shorter tour in 1967 which still included 17 matches of which the All Blacks won 16, only East Wales denying them when holding out for a 3–3 draw in Cardiff. Any victory over New Zealand deserves nothing less than the highest praise and the accolades that are inevitably bestowed on the winning team. Perhaps it is somewhat churlish to make comparisons but, when looking at the records, one begins to understand why those in Newport and even Cardiff and Swansea get a little miffed when Llanelli's famous day is recognised above all others – I blame Max Boyce!

Max did the Scarlets proud. His words tell of the famous day in a way no other poet, singer-songwriter or troubadour could have hoped to capture. Max got it right, he hit the button with words that soar, bring a smile to the face, a tear to the eye. You didn't have to come from Llanelli or even be Welsh to enjoy the piece titled simply '9–3'. To listen to the tale of how the pubs ran dry, the bloodshot absentees, the doctors' papers and the scoreboard which informed Llanelli 9 Seland Newydd 3, all make for an uplifting experience, but it doesn't tell the full story. Passing reference is made to a handful of

Llanelli players but the real issue is not how wonderfully well the Scarlets played or how they were expertly coached by the astute Carwyn James in this the club's centenary season. What tends to be overlooked regarding this most famous day is the make-up of the New Zealand team. Ian Kirkpatrick, Andy Haden, Peter Whiting, Bryan Williams and Bruce Robertson were outstanding All Blacks which is confirmed by the number of Test appearances they each made, but elsewhere it is a very different story. The remaining ten players mustered together a mere 47 caps between them. Even if names such as Bob Burgess, Joe Karam and Alan Sutherland are included amongst them this is a poor return and reflects the lack of international experience evident on the day, a detail compounded when one notes that Karam and Sutherland each won ten caps. No, this was not a great New Zealand team, but we should not lose sight of the fact that there is never a bad one, just that some are better than others.

On subsequent tours Munster, England's Northern Division and Midland Division were added to the list of teams that defeated New Zealand. If we take it as read that 1997 was the last time the All Blacks undertook a tour of Britain that extended beyond international fixtures, then we are able to draw a line and assess all that had gone before. This gives us 15 tours to consider and a total of 307 matches played of which 278 were won. I suspect every reader will know where this is heading, but bear with me. With ten matches drawn this leaves 19 losses of which eight were against international opposition. Four English regions each had their day as did one in France and an Irish province prevailed, so too did the star studded Barbarians – which leaves four.

The four Welsh clubs should head any list because they each took on New Zealand independently. The players wore some famous jerseys: the white of Swansea, Cardiff's blue and black, the black and amber of Newport, and the scarlet of Llanelli. Four great clubs who each downed the might of New Zealand, achievements that have never been replicated and never will be. Now that really is something for Welsh rugby to celebrate, despite the national team's failure to beat New Zealand in a period that has extended to 60 years and counting. Perhaps now is the time to lay the argument to rest, call it a draw, let Wales' most famous clubs revel in the glory bestowed on them by those who have gone before. What a cop-out that would be! Having got so far we will find a performance that stands out above all others – now is their hour and they are entitled to enjoy every second of it.

Newport RFC were the only side to defeat the 1963–4 New Zealand All Blacks. The club succeeded where 35 other teams failed. Not only did Newport win the match but was, without doubt, the better side on the day. This against an All Blacks side that in Wilson Whineray boasted the man widely regarded as New Zealand's finest captain; Colin Meads, New Zealand's player of the century; Don Clarke, the greatest goal kicker the game had seen at the time; and in Waka Nathan, Kel Tremain and Brian Lochore, a back row that would be more than comfortable in the modern game. That the team failed to match such legendary status in other departments is irrelevant, but it would have been damn near impossible to do so. Players of the calibre of Ian Clarke, John Major, Ron Horsley, Kevin Briscoe, Earle Kirton, Pat Walsh, Ian MacRae, Bill Davis and Ralph Caulton have to stand up and be counted a little further down the pecking order, such is the way of the world.

This was a mighty New Zealand team that were comprehensively outplayed on the day by a Newport team that raised the bar for all that would follow. Barring the drawn international against Scotland, the fifth All Blacks won all 34 of the remaining fixtures and when they returned home, the players could hold their heads high in the knowledge that only the Invincibles in 1924–5 and the 1905–06 All Blacks could claim better records – marginally better records at that.

For a club to defeat such a strong New Zealand team remains one of the finest achievements in the history of rugby union football. Discount international matches and it stands alone. Nothing compares with it and in an era where the game has new agendas and new structures in place, nothing ever will.

Appendix I

W HAT BECAME OF the Newport players who enjoyed a unique, never to be repeated moment together on a wet Wednesday afternoon in October 50 years ago?

RAY CHENEY played two full seasons at Newport, in addition to the two months at the end of the 1962–3 campaign. During his comparatively short stay, the full-back broke the club's points scoring record in 1963–4 and improved on it the following season when scoring 224 points. The break came when Cheney took a twelve-month appointment in Scotland, playing his rugby for Strathclyde and the West of Scotland. Home for Christmas, there was no place for him at Newport and a chance meeting with Cardiff's Dai Hayward saw Ray Cheney exchange the black and amber for the blue and black. A change of job took Cheney north again, to Harrogate where he played under the captaincy of Welsh hooker, Jeff Young. Later Ray Cheney would spend some years in South Africa, during which he played for a veterans' team at the famous Wanderers club in Johannesburg.

For STUART WATKINS the road would also lead to Cardiff, but not before he had enjoyed six seasons with Newport in which he scored 115 tries. Watkins won the first of 26 caps when selected to play against Scotland in 1964, barely three months after the New Zealand match. He represented the British Lions on the tour of Australia and New Zealand in 1966, playing in three Tests. Stuart Watkins later returned to Newport RFC where he served on various committees in the years leading up to the professional era.

Once DENNIS PERROTT had joined the club he had supported as a lad, there would be no getting him away from there. Perrott completed ten successful seasons at Newport, making 207 appearances and scoring 78 tries. At the time of his retirement at 33 years of age, only Keith Poole, the youngest Newport player back in 1963, was still commanding a place in the team. Dennis Perrott is secretary of the Black and Amber Former Players Association.

In six seasons with Newport, DICK UZZELL played 100 matches for the club. A modest return perhaps, but his was a rugby career plagued by injury. After winning his first cap against New Zealand, Uzzell was absent from the Welsh team until 1965 when he played in all four championship matches which included a Triple Crown. Another to take the A48 west, Uzzell joined Cardiff in 1967, and became a stalwart with the Rags, the second XV, and ended his career helping Brian Price bring on the young talent at Caldicot RFC. As for that drop goal? Popular myth has it that Dick Uzzell had never dropped a goal before and would never repeat the effort again. One could be forgiven for thinking this was true when many years later he was interviewed pitch-side for television and invited to try his luck at reproducing the famous act. Time and again Dick failed before, eventually, slotting the ball over. But his effort in 1963 was not the first time he had registered a drop goal for Newport. Records confirm that in the previous season he had one to his credit and in 1965–6 he popped over two more.

BRIAN 'BJ' JONES joined Newport as an 18 year old in 1953. He played for the club through to the end of the 1963–4 season, following which he had two seasons sharing his wealth of experience at Tredegar RFC before returning to Rodney Parade for a swansong that saw him retire from the game in 1968. BJ played 328 games for Newport, including four against major touring teams. He captained the club in consecutive seasons between 1959–61, was club coach between 1967–9 during which time Newport were crowned Welsh club champions, and he went on to perform administrative functions at the club, serving as both secretary and chairman. There were two Welsh caps and, among his appearances for the Barbarians, was the defeat of South Africa in 1961 which gives Jones the rare distinction of having played on a winning club side against each of the major southern hemisphere countries.

DAVID WATKINS was one of the union game's true superstars. Not satisfied with that, he broke ranks, joined Salford RLFC and became one of rugby league's superstars. There were 21 Welsh caps, including three appearances as captain and six Test appearances with the British Lions in 1966 – Watkins leading the team against New Zealand in the second and fourth Tests. In his twelve seasons at Salford, he scored 3,117 points in 472 games, became a dual Welsh international and was capped six times by Great Britain. Watkins was elected Newport captain in four consecutive seasons, 1964–8, but his tenure was cut short when he turned professional in October 1967. When rugby union became a professional sport in 1995, the strict regulations regarding amateurism were relaxed and David Watkins returned to Newport as a board member of the newly-formed company and went on to serve as chairman and president. He was one of twelve inductees at the inaugural dinner celebrating the Newport Hall of Fame in 2012.

Watkins' half-back partner for much of the four seasons between 1961–5 was BOB PROSSER. Never to play for Wales due to Clive Rowlands' selection as Welsh captain for 14 consecutive matches, Prosser was able to concentrate on his club rugby and, after making 29 first-team appearances in his first season, he put together an impressive run that saw him don the number nine jersey in no fewer than 118 of the 135 matches Newport played between September 1962 and April 1965. If the rugby league scouts wanted any confirmation that this short, compact player would be able to cope with the perceived increased physicality of the game up north, this was it. Bob Prosser signed professional papers with St Helens RLFC in the summer of 1965 and joined Salford RLFC when that club signed David Watkins two years later. Bob Prosser played rugby at varying levels until the age of 48, when a broken arm finally forced him to hang up his boots. He still resides in the north of England.

NEVILLE JOHNSON spent nine seasons at Rodney Parade before a back injury brought his playing career to a premature end. There may well have been some fuel left in the tank, but prop forwards and back injuries do not sit comfortably together. Twenty years later Johnson would join forces with former Newport, Wales and British Lions three-quarter Gareth Evans as the club's coaching team. Nev Johnson now lives in Spain where he is one of another duo. Guitar at the ready he can be found entertaining ex-pats on the club circuit.

For hooker GRAHAM BEVAN it had been a waiting game before he was able to claim the position in the middle of the front row as his own. Over nine seasons he played almost 200 matches for the club, most of them in the four years he remained with Newport following the retirement of Bryn Meredith. Known as a staunch Labour supporter and union man, Graham Bevan was the first member of the Newport team to pass away, dying in May 1995.

DAVID JONES was another who had to show great patience before becoming a regular first-team player. He spent two seasons during which Des Greenslade was preferred, before getting his chance in 1963–4 when he appeared in 42 of the 48 matches. The following season, which would be his last at Newport, Jones only made two appearances before leaving to join Tredegar. This marked change in fortune was never satisfactorily explained, but David Jones knows that when it came to the biggest game of them all, his name was on the team sheet.

At 34 years of age, IAN FORD was the senior member of the Newport team, but that counted for nothing on the day. Capped twice by Wales in 1959, Ford is best remembered at Rodney Parade as a one-time holder of the club's record for the number of appearances, 482 over 17 seasons. His agricultural background saw him emigrate to New Zealand, where he spent five years working for the Ministry of Horticulture. Based in the Bay of Islands, Ford's brief was simply to teach the Kiwis to grow kiwi fruit. On his return to Britain, he spent some time in Guernsey before eventually settling in Kent where he still lives. Ian Ford was inducted into the Newport Hall of Fame in 2013.

Newport captain against New Zealand was **BRIAN PRICE**. His ten seasons at Rodney Parade ended with a second term of office in 1968–9, a season which saw Newport crowned Welsh club champions. The record books were rewritten – Newport playing a thrilling brand of rugby that brought plaudits wherever the club appeared. Winner of 32 caps, Price led Wales six times and was a member of the British Lions team that toured Australia and New Zealand in 1966. He returned three years later when he captained the first Welsh team to tour those countries. The All Blacks included some familiar faces with Ian MacRae, Kel Tremain, Waka Nathan and Colin Meads playing against the Lions and MacRae, Bill Davis, Earle Kirton and Meads against Wales. Having taken over the captaincy from the retired Wilson Whineray, Brian Lochore led the All Blacks in the whitewash against the Lions, and was still captain when Wales visited.

Brian Price played against New Zealand seven times: for Wales in 1963 and the two Tests in 1969, two Tests for the British Lions in 1966, and he represented the Barbarians against the fifth All Blacks in 1964. All these matches ended in defeat, but the picture changes when we include the day he led Newport on what was his 26th birthday and when he received the best present imaginable.

When **ALAN 'ALGY' THOMAS** tackled Bill Davis into touch at the corner flag in what was the final piece of play on 30 October, his first reaction was "where the **** was Poolie!" Algy had packed on the right side of the last scrum which was set under the posts. The All Blacks took play to Newport's left, but that he was there when it mattered says all one needs to know about this most competitive of wing-forwards. Capped twice by Wales, Algy made 212 appearances for Newport before moving on to Neath, Ebbw Vale and finally Cross Keys. On a trade delegation to New Zealand some years later, he was entertained by Wilson Whineray at his home and returned the compliment when Whineray's daughter visited Britain.

GLYN DAVIDGE may well have played his finest game against New Zealand, but those who saw Newport play South Africa in 1961 recall an equally magnificent performance. Davidge was fearless and enjoyed nothing more than getting among the opposing forwards, doing the hard graft on the floor regardless of any risk to life and limb. He gained international recognition winning nine Welsh caps and was a replacement for the British Lions when they toured South Africa in 1962. Captain of Newport in 1962–3, Davidge made 270 appearances for the club. The second of the Newport team to pass away, Glyn Davidge died on 18 March 2006.

A quick look at the footage would tell Algy Thomas that KEITH POOLE was not far away. This was the day a boy became a man and over the next 15 years he would make a total of 486 appearances for Newport, breaking Ian Ford's record in the process. These included the drawn match with Australia in 1966, the victory over the Springboks in 1969, and a second meeting with the All Blacks in 1973 which ended in defeat. High on the list of achievements during the period is Newport's 16–15 victory over Cardiff in the 1977 Welsh Cup final in which Poole stopped the mighty Gareth Edwards from scoring what looked to be a certain try with a bone-crunching tackle that shook the stadium – have a look at that one Algy!

Appendix II

Newport RFC Results – 1963

2 March	Cardiff	A	W	6–5
9 March	Wasps	A	W	15–0
13 March	Llanelli	H	W	5–0
16 March	Aberavon	A	W	9–8
20 March	Penarth	H	W	16–6
23 March	Gloucester	A	L	3–8
27 March	Cardiff	H	D	8–8
30 March	Neath	H	W	9–3
4 April	Swansea	A	L	3–5
6 April	Bridgend	H	W	22–8
8 April	Ebbw Vale	H	W	19–3
13 April	Newbridge	H	W	3–0
15 April	L. Welsh	H	W	14–3
16 April	Barbarians	H	W	16–15
20 April	Plymouth	A	W	17–5
22 April	Devonport Services	A	W	33–9
23 April	Exeter	A	W	32–9
7 Sept	Roma	H	D	8–8
9 Sept	Penarth	H	W	23–0
14 Sept	Bristol	A	L	0–16
21 Sept	Neath	A	L	11–22
25 Sept	Gloucester	H	W	6–3
28 Sept	Swansea	H	D	8–8
2 Oct	Aberavon	H	W	8–5
5 Oct	Cardiff	H	L	6–14
12 Oct	Blackheath	A	W	10–3
16 Oct	Pontypool	H	W	13–0

19 Oct	Gloucester	A	L	3–14
26 Oct	Wasps	H	W	11–0
30 Oct	New Zealand	H	W	3–0
2 Nov	Ebbw Vale	H	W	12–0
9 Nov	Cardiff	A	L	0–3
16 Nov	Camb. Univ.	A	L	0–14
20 Nov	Ebbw Vale	A	L	0–6
23 Nov	L. Welsh	A	W	19–12
30 Nov	Llanelli	H	W	26–5
7 Dec	Bristol	H	W	9–3
10 Dec	Comb. Serv.	H	W	15–6
13 Dec	Aberavon	A	W	6–0
26 Dec	Watsonians	H	W	25–11
27 Dec	UAU	H	W	13–5
28 Dec	Cross Keys	A	W	14–3

Played 42 Won 30 Drew 3 Lost 9

Appendix III

New Zealand Tour Results 1963–4

23 Oct	Oxford University, Oxford	W	19–3
26 Oct	Southern Counties, Hove	W	32–3
30 Oct	Newport, Newport	L	0–3
2 Nov	Aberavon & Neath, Port Talbot	W	11–6
6 Nov	Abertillery & Ebbw Vale, Abertillery	W	13–0
9 Nov	London Counties, Twickenham	W	27–0
13 Nov	Cambridge University, Cambridge	W	20–6
16 Nov	South of Scotland, Hawick	W	8–0
20 Nov	Glasgow & Edinburgh, Glasgow	W	33–3
23 Nov	Cardiff, Cardiff	W	6–5
27 Nov	Pontypool & Cross Keys, Pontypool	W	11–0
30 Nov	South-Western Counties, Exeter	W	38–6
3 Dec	Midland Counties, Coventry	W	37–9
7 Dec	Ireland, Dublin	W	6–5
11 Dec	Munster, Limerick	W	6–3
14 Dec	Swansea, Swansea	W	16–9
17 Dec	Western Counties, Bristol	W	22–14
21 Dec	Wales, Cardiff	W	6–0
26 Dec	Combined Services, Twickenham	W	23–9
28 Dec	Midland Counties, Leicester	W	14–6
31 Dec	Llanelli, Llanelli	W	22–8
4 Jan	England, Twickenham	W	14–0
8 Jan	North-Western Counties, Manchester	W	12–3
11 Jan	North-Eastern Counties, Harrogate	W	17–11
14 Jan	North of Scotland, Aberdeen	W	15–3
18 Jan	Scotland, Murrayfield	D	0–0
22 Jan	Leinster, Dublin	W	11–8

25 Jan	Ulster, Belfast	W	24–5
29 Jan	South-Eastern Counties, Bournemouth	W	9–6
1 Feb	France B, Toulouse	W	17–8
5 Feb	South-West France, Bordeaux	W	23–0
8 Feb	France, Paris	W	12–3
12 Feb	South-Eastern France, Lyon	W	8–5
15 Feb	Barbarians, Cardiff	W	36–3
22 Feb	British Columbia U25 Xv, Vancouver	W	6–3
24 Feb	British Columbia, Vancouver	W	39–3

Played 36 Won 34 Drew 1 Lost 1

Bibliography

Billot, John, *History of Welsh International Rugby*, Roman Way Books, 1999.

Bond, Karen, Alex Morton and John Griffiths (eds), *The IRB World Rugby Yearbook 2013*, Vision Sports, 2012.

Chester, Rod, Neville McMillan and Ron Palenski, *The Encyclopaedia of New Zealand Rugby*, Hodder Moa Beckett, 1998.

—, *Men in Black*, Hodder Moa Beckett, 2000.

Davenport-Hines, Richard, *An English Affair – Sex, Class and Power in the Age of Profumo*, HarperPress, 2013.

Davis, Haydn, *The History of the Borough of Newport*, Pennyfarthing Press, 1998.

Davis, Jack, *One Hundred Years of Newport Rugby*, Starling Press, 1974.

DeGroot, Gerard, *The '60s Unplugged – A Kaleidoscopic History of a Disorderly Decade*, Macmillan, 2008.

Evans, Howard, *Welsh International Matches 1881–2000*, Mainstream Publishing, 1999.

Fox, Dave, Ken Bogle and Mark Hoskins, *A Century of the All Blacks in Britain and Ireland*, Tempus Publishing Limited, 2006.

Gadney, C.H. *The History of the Laws of Rugby Union Football 1949–1972*, RFU, 1973.

Griffiths, John, *The Phoenix Book of International Rugby Records*, Phoenix House, 1987.

Jenkins, John M., Duncan Pierce and Timothy Auty, *Who's Who of Welsh International Rugby Players*, Bridge Books, 1991.

McAleer, David, Introduction by, *Top 40 Charts*, Virgin Books, 2009.

Norman, Philip, *Shout! The True Story of the Beatles*, Pan Books, 2004.

Roderick, Alan, *Newport Rugby Greats*, Handpost Books, 1995.

Russell-Pavier, Nick and Stewart Richards, *The Great Train Robbery – Crime of the Century, The Definitive Account*, Weidenfeld & Nicholson, 2012.

Sandbrook, Dominic, *Never Had It So Good – A History of Britain from Suez to the Beatles*, Abacus, 2006.

Smith, David and Gareth Williams, *Fields of Praise*, University of Wales Press, 1980.

Swan, A.C., Read Masters and A.H. Carman (eds), *The Rugby Almanack of New Zealand*, Sporting Publications, various editions.

Thomas, Clem, *The History of the British Lions*, Mainstream Publishing, 1996.

Newspapers and Periodicals

New Zealand Rugby
Rugby World
South Wales Argus
Western Mail

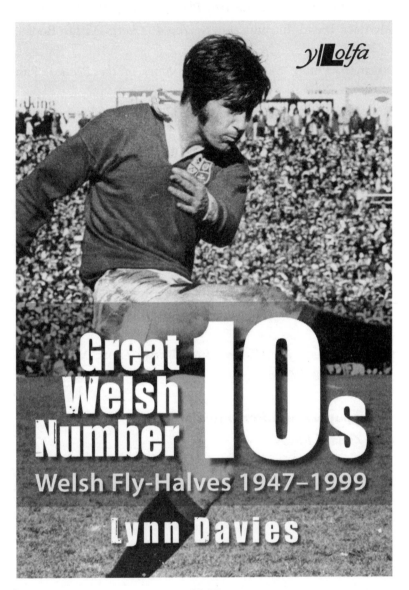